ISRAEL

and the STRUGGLE
over the INTERNATIONAL

LAWS OF WAR

The Hoover Institution gratefully acknowledges the following individuals and foundations for their significant support of the KORET-TAUBE TASK FORCE ON NATIONAL SECURITY AND LAW

Koret Foundation
Tad and Dianne Taube
  Taube Family Foundation
James J. Carroll III
  Jean Perkins Foundation

KORET–TAUBE TASK FORCE ON NATIONAL SECURITY AND LAW

ISRAEL

and the STRUGGLE over the INTERNATIONAL

LAWS OF WAR

Peter Berkowitz

HOOVER INSTITUTION PRESS
STANFORD UNIVERSITY | STANFORD, CALIFORNIA

www.hoover.org

Hoover Institution Press Publication No. 618

Hoover Institution at Leland Stanford Junior University,
Stanford, California, 94305-6010

First printing 2012

18 17 16 15 14 13 12   9 8 7 6 5 4 3 2 1

Manufactured in the United States of America

The paper used in this publication meets the minimum Requirements of the
American National Standard for Information Sciences—Permanence of Paper
for Printed Library Materials, ANSI/NISO Z39.48-1992. ♾

Cataloging-in-Publication Data is available
from the Library of Congress.

ISBN-13: 978-0-8179-1434-9 (cloth)
ISBN-13: 978-0-8179-1436-3 (e-book)

Contents

v

Preface

This short book grew out of the work of the Hoover Institution's Koret-Taube Task Force on National Security and Law, which I chair. The task force was launched five years ago to explore and provide answers to the novel and difficult legal questions that arose in America following al-Qaeda's 9/11 attacks. The distinguished members brought to the task force a variety of opinions and areas of expertise. At the same time, all were in agreement that transnational terrorism presented a grave and long-term threat to the United States, that reconciling the claims of security and liberty was an urgent challenge, and that the US Constitution provided a sturdy and flexible political framework.

From its inception, the task force was devoted to undertaking comparative analysis, and recognized the significance of Israel's experience in fighting terrorism. Since its birth in 1948, Israel has never known a moment in which it was not under immediate threat from terrorist attack. Indeed, no liberal democracy has faced a more sustained assault from non-state enemies. And while Israel has made its share of mistakes, no liberal democracy has acquired greater expertise in defending itself against terrorism while respecting rights and preserving the rule of law.

Israel today stands on the front lines of a new struggle over the international laws of war. In recent years, the term "lawfare" has gained currency to describe the use of international law as a political weapon. Liberal democracies, and in particular Israel and the United States, are the principal targets. They face terrorists who, despite having openly repudiated their own obligations under the international laws of war, undertake with boundless cynicism to exploit the international laws of war to criminalize the right of liberal democracies to defend themselves. At the same time, liberal democracies confront diplomats, human rights lawyers, and United Nations officials who, succumbing to the progressive dream that politics can be replaced by rational administration, exhibit extravagant faith in the ability of diplomats and courts of law to resolve disputes among nations. They aim to rewrite the international laws of war to aggressively reduce the range of circumstances in which states may lawfully use military force. Unfortunately, they leave out of the equation terrorists' resolve, and that of the rogue and authoritarian states that support them, to accomplish their goals by using violence of every conceivable kind against civilians.

The Goldstone report, which was published by the United Nations in September 2009, and the Gaza flotilla controversy, which erupted at the end of May 2010, exemplify lawfare in action. In both cases, in condemnation of actions taken by Israel to defend itself against Hamas— which rules the Gaza Strip, has openly called for Israel's destruction and declared religious war to achieve it, and has targeted civilians as a centerpiece of its military strategy—UN officials, prominent lawyers, and diplomats put forward legal arguments ranging from weak to indefensible. These arguments have enjoyed remarkable influence, especially in Europe, the United States, and even in some precincts in Israel itself. The legal principles and conclusions they advance threaten not only Israel's national security interests but also America's because they work to severely restrict the legitimate use of force by liberal democracies generally. Indeed, many American lawyers, scholars, policy analysts, and government officials already embrace or are well-disposed toward the poor legal reasoning, bound up with faulty political and strategic judgments, advanced by the Goldstone report and in the Gaza flotilla controversy.

The critique of the abuses of the international laws of war should not be confused with rejection or disparagement of the international laws of war. Both the Israeli military and the US military rightly and proudly are devoted to upholding them. As liberal democracies committed to human rights while bearing special responsibility to protect the rights of their own citizens, Israel and America have a vital national security interest in their allies and their adversaries too considering themselves bound by international laws of war that seek to balance the legitimate claims of military necessity and humanitarian responsibility. This book is intended to contribute to the defense of the international laws of war by exposing the flawed assumptions and refuting the defective claims that have gained currency through the Goldstone report and Gaza flotilla controversy.

Early on in puzzling over the Goldstone report, lively conversations with International Committee of the Red Cross legal advisor Nathalie Weizmann suggested fruitful lines of inquiry. My Hoover colleague Emily Messner provided excellent research into the legal issues that lie at the heart of this book and crucial editorial assistance. Once again Linda Berkowitz's proofreading saved me from numerous errors and infelicities of expression.

The main arguments were developed in three articles that appeared in Hoover's *Policy Review*;[1] they all benefited from editor Tod Lindberg's subtle and unobtrusive advice. Professor Gabriella Blum brought just the right mix of skepticism and enthusiasm to many discussions and comments on draft chapters. Professors Robert Howse and Ruti Teitel graciously shared their expertise on international law, patiently answering numerous questions and walking me through a variety of difficult matters. Professor Laurie Blank directed my attention to the complexities involved in applying the key international laws of war principles, distinction and proportionality, to combat operations. Ethics and Public Policy Senior Fellow Stanley Kurtz urged me to keep in mind the larger controversies in which the struggle over the international laws of war is embedded. After hours, Brookings Institution Senior Fellow Ben Wittes and Deputy Assistant Secretary of State Tammy Wittes opened

---

1. "The Goldstone Report and International Law," in *Policy Review,* No. 162, Aug./Sept. 2010, available at http://www.hoover .org/publications/policy-review/article/43281; "The Goldstone Mess," in *Policy Review,* No. 166, April/May 2011, available at http://www .hoover.org/publications/policy-review/article/73356; and "The Gaza Flotilla and International Law," in *Policy Review,* Aug./Sept. 2011, available at http://www.hoover.org/publications/policy-review/article/ 86476. In addition, Chapter 1 draws on and revises "Upon Further Review . . ." in *The Weekly Standard,* April 18, 2011, available at http://www.weeklystandard.com/articles/upon-further-review_5570 17.html. This and all subsequent links accessed Dec. 14, 2011.

their home and provided Scotch and the opportunity to ruminate about matters great and small. I have learned much from my task force colleagues, in formal meetings and casual settings, about the substance and rhetoric of the international laws of war. Professors Kenneth Anderson and Jack Goldsmith were on call around the clock to provide emergency assistance on technical legal puzzles.

Hoover Fellows David Davenport and Abe Sofaer have been good friends of the task force and offered wise counsel on the case of Israel. Hoover Deputy Director David Brady has been an indispensable partner in the task force's conception, launch, and execution. Hoover Business Manager Marianne Jacobi, Assistant Director Denise Elson, and Senior Associate Director Stephen Langlois labored behind the scenes to ensure the task force's smooth functioning. Hoover Director John Raisian gave unstinting encouragement and institutional support. Without the generosity of the Koret Foundation, the Taube Family Foundation, and the Jean Perkins Foundation, neither the task force nor this book would have been possible. Indeed, it has been a great pleasure to work with Koret President and Taube Family Foundation President Tad Taube, Koret CEO Jeffrey Farber, and Jean Perkins Foundation President Jamie Carroll, all of whom immediately grasped the task force's mission, and have encouraged us to vigorously pursue the issues as they come into view.

PETER BERKOWITZ
Washington, DC

CHAPTER ONE

An Opportunity to Reorient

To the astonishment of Israel's friends and foes alike, on April 1, 2011 in the *Washington Post,* below the understated title "Reconsidering the Goldstone Report on Israel and War Crimes," Justice Richard Goldstone reversed himself.[1] Published in September 2009 as the "Report of the United Nations Fact Finding Mission on the Gaza Conflict," the Goldstone report quickly became the proof text for those determined to denounce Israel as an outlaw nation. Accordingly, Israeli Prime Minister Benjamin Netanyahu promptly responded to Goldstone's reconsideration by demanding that the United Nations retract the report. Meanwhile, Goldstone's mission colleagues— London School of Economics professor Christine Chinkin; Colonel Desmond Travers, a former officer in Ireland's Defence Forces; and Supreme Court of Pakistan advocate Hina Jilani—have shown no sign of changing their minds.

---

1. Available at http://www.washingtonpost.com/opinions/reconsider ing-the-goldstone-report-on-israel-and-war-crimes/2011/04/01/ AFg111JC_story.html.

On April 4, three days after the publication of Goldstone's reconsideration, Jilani declared that "no process or acceptable procedure would invalidate the UN Report," and neither she nor the other members have indicated any need to reconsider since.

Yet however determined his colleagues have been to stick to their story and regardless of the failure of the UN to officially repudiate the report, Goldstone's reconsideration is noteworthy. Goldstone withdrew the gravest charge that he and his colleagues had leveled against Israel and its three-week Gaza operation of December 2008–January 2009, which aimed at stopping Hamas's firing of thousands of mortar shells, rockets, and missiles at civilian populations in southern Israel. According to Goldstone— former justice of the Constitutional Court of South Africa and former prosecutor of the International Criminal Tribunals for the former Yugoslavia and for Rwanda—it is now well established, both by Israeli military investigations and by "the final report by the UN committee of independent experts" (chaired by former New York judge Mary McGowan Davis) that "civilians were not intentionally targeted as a matter of policy" by Israel. Coming from Goldstone—chosen to head the Human Rights Council's investigation in part because of the prestige he brought as a leading figure among international human rights lawyers—this exoneration was as welcome as it was unexpected. But, like much else in his *Post* piece, it was partial and misleading.

Goldstone wrote as if he were confronting a lingering suspicion that finally could be laid to rest. He failed to acknowledge that nothing had done more than the UN mission he led and the report it issued—endorsed by the UN General Assembly in November 2009 by a vote of 114 to 18, with 44 countries abstaining—to promulgate the slander that Israel had adopted an essentially criminal strategy in Operation Cast Lead.

In fact, the Goldstone report culminates with the legal finding—not a factual finding or suspicion but a legal conclusion—that in the Gaza conflict Israel undertook "a deliberately disproportionate attack designed to punish, humiliate and terrorize a civilian population, radically diminish its local economic capacity both to work and to provide for itself, and to force upon it an ever increasing sense of dependency and vulnerability."[2]

With this calumny, the Goldstone report went beyond asserting a moral equivalence between Israel and the terrorists it was fighting. It affirmed that Israel was worse than Hamas, since Israel was a state, since Israel used state-of-the-art weaponry, and since the death and destruction it supposedly deliberately inflicted on civilians in Gaza was much greater in raw numbers than the harm to civilians in southern Israel caused by eight years of Hamas bombardment.

In the *Washington Post*, Goldstone obliquely blamed his report's most egregious errors on Israel's refusal to cooperate: "The allegations of intentionality by Israel were based on the deaths of and injuries to civilians in situations where our fact-finding mission had no evidence on which to draw

---

2. Goldstone report, Part V, par. 1690, available at http://www2 .ohchr.org/english/bodies/hrcouncil/specialsession/9/docs/unffmgc_ report.pdf.

any other reasonable conclusion." This is incorrect. For one thing, Goldstone and his colleagues did not leave matters at "allegations"; they made numerous legal findings that Israel, as a matter of strategy and policy, targeted civilians. For another, it was not as Goldstone now contends that he and his team lacked evidence to avoid the conclusion of intentionality. Rather, the evidence he and his team collected and on which they based their legal findings was *always* insufficient to reasonably reach the conclusion that the Israel Defense Forces (IDF) had committed war crimes and crimes against humanity.

The relevant body of law is international humanitarian law, a part of the international laws of war that "seeks to limit the effects of armed conflict" and is also known as the laws of war or the law of armed conflict.[3] To find that a military has used unlawful or disproportionate force, the international laws of war require an analysis of the understandings and intentions of commanders and soldiers and a determination of whether their decisions and conduct were reasonable in the circumstances. The Goldstone report contains no such analysis, in significant measure because it lacked information about the understandings and intentions of Israeli commanders and soldiers. True, Israel declined to cooperate, but it was under no legal obligation to do so. The Goldstone report, moreover, was, as a matter of law, precluded from inferring criminal intent either from Israel's decision not to cooperate or from the absence of informa-

---

3. "What is International Humanitarian Law?" International Committee of the Red Cross Advisory Service on International Humanitarian Law," available at http://www.icrc.org/eng/assets/files/other/what_is_ihl.pdf. I will generally use the broader term "international laws of war."

tion about Israeli understandings and intentions. Nevertheless the Goldstone report leapt to grim legal conclusions about the use of disproportionate force without such elementary information as the rules of engagement under which IDF commanders and soldiers operated. Such information was critical because Israel's terrorist adversaries relentlessly sought to blur the distinction—fundamental to the international laws of war—between civilians and combatants by unlawfully positioning themselves in densely populated areas and unlawfully fighting without uniforms. In short, the Goldstone report's legal finding that Israel sought to "terrorize a civilian population" was based on inadequate factual findings and so was inherently invalid.

Goldstone's reconsideration also withdrew—without making clear it was doing so—a scurrilous charge against the Israeli legal system. It cited approvingly the McGowan Davis report, which notes that "'Israel has dedicated significant resources to investigate over 400 allegations of operational misconduct in Gaza' while 'the de facto authorities (i.e., Hamas) have not conducted any investigations into the launching of rocket and mortar attacks against Israel.'"

In rightly crediting Israel's investigations, however, Goldstone omits mention of his report's baseless finding that Israel's system of civilian and military justice "does not comply with" the principles of international law.[4] The Goldstone report reached this damning conclusion even though Israel's procedures for investigating war crimes allegations compare favorably with, and in important respects

4. Goldstone report, Part IV, par. 1612.

are more exacting than, those of the United States, Canada, the United Kingdom, and Australia.

Some distinguished Israelis, including *Haaretz* journalist Aluf Benn and Hebrew University of Jerusalem Professor Shlomo Avineri, have argued that an important lesson to be learned from Goldstone's reconsideration is that Israel ought to have cooperated with the Goldstone mission and should cooperate with similar international investigations in the future.[5] Even if the investigators are biased, better for Israel to make its case and get it on record before official conclusions are published and ratified by the UN.

That is the wrong lesson. Israel should not acquiesce to one set of rules and standards for itself and another for all other states. Under the international laws of war, the right and the obligation to investigate and prosecute war crimes belongs in the first place to the nations accused. Only when a country has shown itself unwilling or unable to exercise its right and discharge its obligation are international bodies authorized to pursue war crimes investigations. In fact, Israel, whose devotion to the international laws of war is something of which its soldiers and citizens should be proud, was following established procedures

---

5. See Benn, "Goldstone retraction shows West's changed attitude toward Israel in light of Arab world turmoil," in *Haaretz*, April 3, 2011, available at http://www.haaretz.com/print-edition/news/goldstone-retraction-shows-west-s-changed-attitude-toward-israel-in-light-of-arab-world-turmoil-1.353732. And see Avineri, "Israel was wrong to boycott Goldstone probe," in *Haaretz*, April 6, 2011, available at http://www.haaretz.com/print-edition/opinion/israel-was-wrong-to-boycott-goldstone-probe-1.354359.

and in the early stages of its investigations when the Goldstone team began work. Israel should not cooperate in the abrogation of its rights and responsibilities as a sovereign nation.

The right lesson is that Israel must continue to cultivate respect for the international laws of war while vigorously championing a sound understanding of them at home and abroad. Indeed, the Goldstone reconsideration provides an excellent opportunity to reorient public discussion, and not only for Israel but also for the United States, which, like its only liberal and democratic ally in the Middle East, is locked in a long war against transnational terrorists.

The international laws of war arise out of the determination to strike a reasonable balance between military necessity and humanitarian responsibility. These can be mutually supportive: in repelling aggression an army in the first place aims to protect its own civilians. But very often they collide as armies seek to defeat their opponents with the smallest cost to themselves in blood and treasure, which can readily result in unintended harm to the other side's civilians and civilian objects. Giving both military necessity and humanitarian responsibility their due is the hard task and worthy ambition of the international laws of war.

Goldstone rightly observes at the end of his reconsideration that "the laws of armed conflict apply no less to non-state actors such as Hamas than they do to national armies." It's high time to recognize that the chief threat to international law and order comes not, as many western intellectuals and international human rights lawyers are inclined to believe, from Israel and the United States, whose militaries devote untold and unprecedented hours to studying and enforcing the laws of war, but from the terrorists, who utterly reject them. And it's also high time to recognize that in our age the struggle over the international laws of war has become critical to the defense of liberal democracy in a dangerous world, and therefore critical to the US-Israel partnership.

CHAPTER TWO

The Goldstone Report

The controversy over the "Report of the United Nations Fact Finding Mission on the Gaza Conflict"[1] (September 15, 2009), more commonly known as the Goldstone report, has died down. Yet notwithstanding Justice Goldstone's April 2011 reconsideration and partial retraction in the *Washington Post*,[2] the report's far-reaching defects and their implications for the international laws of war have yet to be fully appreciated.

For the most part, the controversy has swirled around the reliability of the Goldstone report's factual findings and the validity of its legal findings concerning Operation Cast Lead, which Israel launched against Hamas fighters in the Gaza Strip on December 27, 2008, and concluded

---

1. Available at http://www2.ohchr.org/english/bodies/hrcouncil/specialsession/9/docs/unffmgc_report.pdf.

2. "Reconsidering the Goldstone Report on Israel and War Crimes," in *The Washington Post*, April 1, 2011, available at http://www.washingtonpost.com/opinions/reconsidering-the-goldstone-report-on-israel-and-war-crimes/2011/04/01/AFg111JC_story.html.

9

on January 18, 2009. But another and more far-reaching issue, which should be of great importance to those who take seriously the claims of international law to govern the conduct of war, has scarcely been noticed. And that pertains to the disregarding of fundamental norms and principles of international law by the United Nations Human Rights Council (HRC), which authorized the Goldstone mission; by the mission members, who produced the Goldstone report; and by the HRC and the United Nations General Assembly (of which the HRC is a subsidiary organ), which endorsed the report's recommendations. Their conduct combines an exaltation of, and disrespect for, international law. It is driven by an ambition to shift authority over critical judgments about the conduct of war from states to international institutions. This shift impairs the ability of liberal democracies to deal lawfully and effectively with the complex and multifarious threats presented by transnational terrorists.

Notwithstanding a veneer of equal interest in the unlawful conduct of both Israel and the Palestinians, the Goldstone report overwhelmingly focused on allegations that in Operation Cast Lead Israel committed war crimes and crimes against humanity. The purpose of Israel's three-week operation was to substantially reduce the mortar shells, rockets, and missiles that Hamas, long recognized by the United States and the European Union as a terrorist organization, had been unlawfully raining down upon civilian targets in southern Israel for eight years. Hamas had intensified these attacks following its victory in the January 2006 Palestinian Legislative Council elections over its rival Fatah, and its subsequent bloody expulsion of Fatah and total takeover of Gaza from the Palestinian Authority in

June 2007. While the Goldstone report recognized that the targeting of Israeli civilians by Palestinian armed groups constituted war crimes and indicated that here and there Palestinians may have committed war crimes during the Gaza operation, it purported to find substantial evidence—based primarily on the testimony of Palestinians either affiliated with, or subject to, Hamas—that Israel had repeatedly violated international law by using disproportionate force. At its most incendiary, the Goldstone report found that Israel committed crimes against humanity—the gravest breaches of international law—by implementing a deliberate policy of terrorizing Palestinian civilians and destroying civilian infrastructure.[3]

Israel has provided three major responses to the Goldstone report. In March 2010 the Intelligence and Terrorism Information Center (ITIC), an Israeli NGO that works closely with the Israel Defense Forces (IDF), published and posted online a 349-page study, "Hamas and the Terrorist Threat from the Gaza Strip: The Main Findings of the Goldstone Report Versus the Factual Findings."[4] Like the two previously published accounts by the Israeli government of the country's continuing investigations of allegations of unlawful conduct committed by its armed forces during the three weeks of Operation Cast Lead—"The Operation in Gaza: Factual and Legal Aspects" (July 29,

---

3. As I discussed in Chapter 1, in his reconsideration, Goldstone withdrew the gravest charge, concluding that "civilians were not intentionally targeted as a matter of policy" by Israel. See http://www.washingtonpost.com/opinions/reconsidering-the-goldstone-report-on-israel-and-war-crimes/2011/04/01/AFg111JC_story.html.

4. Available at http://www.terrorism-info.org.il/malam_multimedia/English/eng_n/pdf/g_report_e1.pdf.

2009),[5] and "Gaza Operation Investigations: An Update" (January 29, 2010)[6]—it garnered next to no attention in the press, from international human rights organizations, from the HRC, or from the General Assembly. Nor have the Goldstone report's champions in the international human rights community or Justice Goldstone and his colleagues dealt seriously with the incisive criticisms published by scholars and journalists of both the report's factual and legal findings.[7]

But the deeper issue for international law concerns the right and the responsibility of states to make lawful judgments about the conduct of war, including the crucial judgments in asymmetric warfare concerning what con-

---

5. Available at http://www.mfa.gov.il/NR/rdonlyres/E89E699D-A435-491B-B2D0-017675DAFEF7/0/GazaOperation.pdf.

6. Available at http://www.mfa.gov.il/NR/rdonlyres/8E841A98-1755-413D-A1D2-8B30F64022BE/0/GazaOperationInvestigations Update.pdf.

7. See, for example, the articles gathered in *The Goldstone Report "Reconsidered": A Critical Analysis,* ed. Gerald M. Steinberg and Anne Nerzberg (Jerusalem: NGO Monitor and Jerusalem Center for Public Affairs, 2011); "Opportunity Missed," *Economist,* September 17, 2009, available at http://goldstonereport.org/pro-and-con/critics/308-the-economist-opportunity-missed; Joshua Muravchik, "Goldstone: An Exegesis," *World Affairs,* May/June 2010, available at http://www.worldaffairsjournal.org/articles/2010-MayJune/full-Muravchik-Traub-MJ-2010.html; Richard Landes, "Goldstone's Gaza Report: Part One: A Failure of Intelligence" and "Goldstone Gaza Report: Part Two: A Miscarriage of Human Rights," *Meria,* December 2009, available at http://www.gloria-center.org/2009/12/landes1-2009-12-01/ and http://www.gloria-center.org/2009/12/landes2-2009-12-02/; Asa Kasher, "Operation Cast Lead and the Ethics of Just War," available at http://www.azure.org.il/article.php?id=502; and Keith Pavlischek, "Proportionality in Warfare," *New Atlantis* Spring 2010, available at http://www.thenewatlantis.com/publications/proportionality-in-warfare.

stitutes a proportional use of force. That issue cannot be resolved by showing that the Goldstone report's findings of fact about the Gaza operation are severely biased, or by demonstrating that the report misunderstood and misapplied the test for determining whether Israel exercised force in a proportional manner, although such showings and demonstrations are highly relevant. Nor can it be resolved by bringing to light how the Goldstone mission itself—as conceived and authorized by the Human Rights Council, carried out by Goldstone and his colleagues, and endorsed by the United Nations General Assembly—disregarded basic norms and principles of international law, even though this leads to the heart of the matter. In the end, whether nation-states or international authorities should have primary responsibility for enforcing the lawful conduct of war turns on conflicting opinions about armed conflict, politics, and justice. Even those many conservatives and progressives who share a commitment to the freedom and dignity of the individual may come to different conclusions grounded in divergent views about the best means for securing individual rights while maintaining international order.

Still, long-established rules and practice are clear. Authoritative sources in international law assign primary responsibility for judgments about whether war has been conducted in accordance with the international laws of war to the judicial and other relevant organs of nation-states. That assignment is rooted in the larger liberal tradition's teaching that nation-states—particularly liberal democracies, which are devoted to securing individual rights and are based on the consent of the governed—are the best and most legitimate means of achieving peace, preserving political freedom, and exercising authority over the individual. And that teaching supposes that states are likely to be more sober in assessing their actions and those of other states than are international organizations because states must bear the burden of any reform or rule, or failure to reform and impose rules.

In contrast, the Goldstone report and its supporters appear to be animated by the conviction that judgments about the lawful conduct of war are best and primarily vindicated by international institutions, because of their supposed superior objectivity, impartiality, and expertise. Yet the authors of the Goldstone report and the international institutions they champion have shown themselves, in the guise of applying the law, willing to suppress or skew the facts and ignore the international laws of war as they are in order to remake them as they believe they should be. The report's stunning defects provide one compelling reason to prefer the allocation of responsibilities in international law as it currently stands to the Goldstone report's efforts to transform it. They illustrate that those who are responsible for the operation of international institutions are no less subject to the passions and prejudices that thwart the impartial and objective administration of law than judges and other officials in legal systems in liberal democracies, and in some cases may be more subject to such passions and prejudices.

Israel's Critique of the Goldstone Report

In July 2009, the Israeli foreign ministry published and posted online an analysis of the Gaza operation that was designed to rebut in advance the main charges put forth by the Goldstone report, which would not be released until mid-September. Prepared while Israel was still conducting preliminary field investigations into allegations of unlawful conduct by the IDF, "The Operation in Gaza: Factual and Legal Aspects" covered numerous issues. The 159-page document emphasized Israel's right and obligation under international law to use military force to stop Hamas's bombardment of civilian targets in southern Israel with mortar shells, rockets, and missiles—approximately 12,000 since the year 2000 and 3,000 in 2008 alone. It reported that by late 2008 Hamas had put one million Israeli civilians in range of its weapons and had assembled armed forces of more than 20,000. It described the considerable efforts Israel undertook, in accordance with the UN Charter, to bring international pressure to bear on Hamas, "including urgent appeals to the UN Secretary General and successive Presidents of the Security Council to take determined action, and diplomatic overtures, directly and through intermediaries, to stop the violence." It reaffirmed Israel's adherence to the international laws of war and human rights law and explained that under a proper understanding of both and taking into account Hamas's systematic use of human shields and relentless blurring of the distinction between civilians and combatants, Israel's military operation in Gaza was a proportional response. It provided clear evidence, including photographs and video, that, in flagrant violation of international law, Hamas deliberately engaged in "the launching of rocket attacks from within densely populated areas near schools and protected UN facilities, the commandeering of hospitals as bases of operations and ambulances for transport, the storage of weapons in mosques, and the booby-trapping of entire civilian neighbourhoods so that an attack on one structure would devastate many others." It reviewed the extensive and unprecedented precautions the IDF took to minimize noncombatant casualties—including making hundreds of thousands of phone calls to Gaza residents to warn of impending air strikes—against an adversary that placed civilians in the line of fire as part of a coldly calculated military strategy. It summarized the steps the IDF took during the three-week conflict to ensure the daily delivery of humanitarian supplies to Gaza's civilian population. It acknowledged that "the Gaza Operation resulted in many civilian deaths and injuries and significant damage to public and private property in Gaza." And it reported that the IDF was conducting field investigations into accusations of unlawful conduct against its officers and soldiers; it detailed Israel's extensive and well-established system of military justice of which those investigations were the first stage; and it reaffirmed Israel's right and responsibility under international law to investigate accusations that its military had acted unlawfully and, where appropriate, prosecute and punish war crimes.

"The Operation in Gaza: Factual and Legal Aspects" fell on deaf ears, including those of the Goldstone mission. While complaining that the Israeli government refused to cooperate with its investigation, the Goldstone report virtually ignored Israel's 159-page official statement, packed with critical facts and pertinent legal analysis and available online to all the world.[8]

---

8. Justice Goldstone contended that Israel's refusal to cooperate with his mission was the cause of "any omission" of "information and evidence" concerning "actions by Hamas or other Palestinians groups in Gaza." See his letter of October 29, 2009, to Representative Howard Berman, chairman of the House Committee on Foreign

The second major official statement by the Israeli government, "Gaza Operation Investigations: An Update" (January 29, 2010), was prepared in response to a request from UN Secretary General Ban Ki-moon.[9] A good part of the 46-page document sketched Israel's military justice system and the role of the Attorney General and Supreme Court in overseeing it; how complaints of unlawful conduct in war are brought in Israel; the role of the military advocate general in screening, reviewing, and referring cases; the conduct of command investigations, which evaluate the performance of forces in the field and which yield information relevant to unlawful conduct; the mechanics of criminal investigations and prosecutions; and the substantial similarity of Israel's multilayered system to those of the United Kingdom, United States, Australia, and Canada.[10] In passing, the update noted that "Under inter-

---

Affairs, and Representative Ileana Ros-Lehtinen, ranking member of the House Committee on Foreign Affairs, in response to a US House of Representatives draft resolution condemning the Goldstone report (the Resolution was passed by a large majority on November 3) available at http://law.fordham.edu/faculty/15161.htm. Justice Goldstone's contention is unpersuasive. Besides largely ignoring Israel's publicly available account, which detailed "actions by Hamas or other Palestinian groups in Gaza," Justice Goldstone and his colleagues also neglected publicly available material published by Hamas concerning its unlawful political ambitions and unlawful methods of war. Indeed, they are not a closely guarded secret. A good place to start is Hamas's 1988 covenant, which declares the intention of destroying Israel through religious war, readily available online at http://avalon.law.yale.edu/20th_century/hamas.asp.

9. The discussion of this document draws on Peter Berkowitz, "A Usurpation of National Sovereignty," *National Review Online*, February 10, 2010, available at http://article.nationalreview.com/424501/a-usurpation-of-national-sovereignty/peter-berkowitz.

10. See "Gaza Operation Investigations: An Update," pp. 12–26.

national law, the responsibility to investigate and prosecute alleged violations of the Law of Armed Conflict by a state's military forces falls first and foremost to that state."

In addition, the update indicated that the IDF had launched 150 investigations arising out of the Gaza operation. In the thirty-six that had been referred for criminal investigation, investigators took "evidence from almost 100 Palestinian complainants and witnesses, along with approximately 500 IDF soldiers and commanders." For every one of the thirty-four allegations of harm to civilians or damage to civilian property discussed at length in the Goldstone report, the IDF had initiated an investigation—twenty-two of which the IDF pursued before the report's publication, and twelve of which it pursued after the report aired them.

While no judicial system is perfect, given the substantial similarity of Israel's system for investigating and prosecuting unlawful conduct in war to those of the United Kingdom, United States, Australia, and Canada, it is hard to see how any existing judicial system would be able to pass muster if Israel's were judged inadequate. Yet the Goldstone report found Israel's severely inadequate:

> After reviewing Israel's system of investigation and prosecution of serious violations of human rights and humanitarian law, in particular of suspected war crimes and crimes against humanity, the Mission found major structural flaws that in its view make the system inconsistent with international standards.[11]

---

11. Goldstone report, Part V, Par. 1756.

The Goldstone report reached this extraordinary conclusion without comparing the Israeli system with others, and well before Israel could possibly have made substantial progress in undertaking the investigations—involving not roped-off and locked-down crime scenes but battlefields in enemy territory—of the allegations that arose out of Operation Cast Lead.

The report's harsh judgment might make sense on the supposition that since states are interested parties, their judicial systems should not be assigned responsibility by international law to investigate and prosecute war crimes, an assignment of responsibility which, after all, calls on states to serve as judges in their own cause. In that case, however, the Goldstone report's critique should have been directed not at Israel but at international law itself.

Instead, the Goldstone report cultivates the appearance of applying international law while actually rejecting its imperatives and replacing them with its own. But it does not do so in an evenhanded fashion. Compounding its disregard for law, it evinces little interest in the capability or willingness of Hamas, the governing authority in Gaza, to enforce the international laws of war. Suffice it to say, as Goldstone acknowledged in the *Washington Post,* Hamas has made no discernible effort to investigate war crimes allegations arising out of the Gaza conflict, which should not have been a surprise since Hamas has no discernible system of military justice for discharging its obligation under the international laws of war to do so. And, undermining their claims to be impartial and objective upholders of international law, neither the HRC nor the UN General Assembly nor the greater international human rights community have seemed particularly troubled by this additional failure on the part of Hamas to comply with its legal obligations as the de facto ruler of Gaza.

Israel's January 2010 document also provided rebuttals of Goldstone report factual findings:

- The Goldstone report found that, in the absence of legitimate military objectives, Israel intentionally destroyed the Namar water-wells complex—including pumping machines, pipes, and civil-administration buildings—by air strikes to deprive Gaza's civilian population of clean drinking water. Israel's update, however, furnished photographic evidence demonstrating that the Namar water wells were located inside the walls of a Hamas military compound.

- The Goldstone report found that Israel undertook a "deliberate and premeditated strike" to damage a vacated Gaza wastewater-treatment plant in the al-Sheikh Ejlin neighborhood to cause raw sewage to flow into and destroy farmland. Israel's update, however, indicated that the damage to the plant did not stem from a deliberate IDF attack. The IDF may have damaged the plant inadvertently during a battle with Hamas fighters, or Hamas fighters themselves may have attacked the plant to set loose sewage to hamper the movements of Israeli tanks operating in the area. But "there was no physical evidence or eyewitness testimony to support the conclusion of the Human Rights Council Fact-Finding Report."

- The Goldstone report found that Israel conducted an aerial strike on the el-Bader flour mill to deny Gaza's civilian population the means of providing for their own sustenance and to render them more dependent on Israel. Israel's update, however, pointed out that the Goldstone report contains no evidence that the flour mill was struck from the air; that "photographs of the mill following the incident do not show structural damage consistent with an air attack"; and that the available evidence indicates the flour mill was struck by tank shells during combat operations.

- The Goldstone report found that Israel destroyed the Abu-Askar family home despite its "unmistakably civilian nature." Israel's update, however, maintained that "due to its use as a large storage facility for weapons and ammunition, including Grad missiles, the house of Muhammad Abu-Askar was a legitimate military target." It also emphasized that because the IDF issued warnings to the family to evacuate and delayed the attack until the night, when fewer civilians were present, no civilian casualties ensued.

These are by no means the only examples of doubtful Goldstone report factual findings. Together, they call into the most serious question the reliability of all Goldstone report factual findings.

The unreliability of the report's factual findings, moreover, undercuts the validity of its legal findings. That's because the factual findings are critical to judgments about the central legal questions addressed by the Goldstone report, which concern whether Israel honored the master concepts of the international laws of war governing combat operations: the principle of distinction[12] and the principle of proportionality.[13] The principle of distinction requires parties to a conflict to distinguish between civilians and civilian objects, and combatants and military objects, and prohibits targeting the former. It also requires combatants to distinguish *themselves* from noncombatants—by wearing uniforms, by carrying their arms openly, by not conducting military operations from within civilian areas—so that the other side can uphold its obligations. The principle of proportionality requires that the force used in the pursuit of legitimate military objectives be reasonably expected not to cause harm to civilians or to civilian objects that would be excessive in relation to the anticipated military advantage.

What constitutes a legitimate military objective, what constitutes reasonable expectations, and what constitutes excessive harm to civilians or to civilian objects in relation to anticipated military advantage—indeed, what constitutes a civilian or civilian object in an age of transnational terrorism—can be intensely context-sensitive questions. They will turn not only on difficult-to-determine facts but also on complex military judgments about both sides' strategies and the appropriate tactics on fluid and murky

---

12. ICRC, Customary IHL, Chapter 1, available at http://www
.icrc.org/customary-ihl/eng/docs/v1_cha_chapter1.

13. ICRC, Customary IHL, Rule 14, available at http://www.icrc
.org/customary-ihl/eng/docs/v1_cha_chapter4_rule14.

battlefields. Israeli commanders and soldiers faced extremely hard targeting decisions because Hamas fighters, in violation of the international laws of war, dressed as civilians; hid ammunition, rockets, and missiles in civilian buildings, including schools, hospitals, and mosques; and booby-trapped neighborhoods. To the extent that the Goldstone report got the facts wrong and mischaracterized or downplayed Hamas's strategy and tactics—and the evidence is that it did so egregiously—its legal findings must be rejected.

The Goldstone report not only got facts wrong but also, as Laurie Blank shows in considerable detail, failed to apply the proper legal tests arising out of the principle of distinction and the principle of proportionality.[14] The report concludes that much of the damage caused by Israeli military operations to civilians and ostensibly civilian objects in Gaza involved criminal failure on Israel's part to distinguish them from legitimate military targets. The proper legal test, however, asks whether a reasonable commander in the actual circumstances under scrutiny would believe that the target is being used to make an effective contribution to military actions. The Goldstone report, however, did not obtain information about the understanding and intent of Israeli commanders, including their rules of engagement, because Israel—which was under no legal obligation to do so—declined to cooperate with the Goldstone mission. Nor did the Goldstone mission investi-

---

14. Laurie Blank, "The Application of IHL in the Goldstone Report: A Critical Commentary," *Yearbook of International Humanitarian Law 12* (2009), "Emory Public Law Research Paper No. 10–96," available at http://papers.ssrn.com/sol3/papers.cfm?abstract _id=1596214.

gate Hamas's systematic use of ostensibly civilian objects for military purposes, which causes those objects to lose their immunity. Consequently, the report's many legal findings that Israel failed to properly distinguish civilian objects are inherently invalid.

The report similarly misconceives the fundamental principle of proportionality. Civilian casualties and damage to civilian infrastructure in warfare are not in themselves unlawful or evidence of criminality. Moreover, as I have noted, the standard "excessive" is exceedingly context sensitive, while the legal test of proportionality of which it forms a part involves, as with the test associated with the principle of distinction, a standard of reasonableness. Under the international laws of war, a determination of whether the exercise of force was proportional depends on factual findings about what commanders and soldiers knew and intended, on complex calculations about tactics and strategy, on the care with which decisions were made, on the prudential steps and precautions taken, and on the propriety of sometimes instant judgments in life and death situations. The Goldstone report routinely ignores such legally essential considerations, which vitiates its sensational legal findings.

To be sure, in "Gaza Operation Investigations: An Update," the Israeli government naturally sought to present its judicial system and wartime conduct in the best light, and to set forth the facts and read international law in a manner most favorable to its interests. Therefore, its accounts should be subject to public and professional scrutiny. Regrettably, the update has largely been ignored.

The March 2010 Intelligence and Terrorism Information
Center study, "Hamas and the Terrorist Threat from the
Gaza Strip," focuses on the comprehensive failure of the
Goldstone report to deal with Hamas as the governing
authority of the Gaza Strip and as the main agent in Gaza
undertaking terrorist operations against Israel. Indeed,
except as a target of Israeli or Palestinian Authority violence, the Goldstone report renders invisible Hamas and
the other terrorist organizations operating in Gaza:

> The Report does not refer to them as terrorist organiza-
> tions, but rather calls them "Palestinian armed groups."
> By using such terminology, the Report ignores or at least
> obscures and minimizes the terrorist nature of the organi-
> zations which fire rockets at Israeli civilians (defined by the
> Report as a "war crime"). In fact, the Report does not deal
> with the nature of Hamas and the other terrorist organiza-
> tions in the Gaza Strip at all. It does not mention Hamas'
> ideology (for example, the Hamas Charter, which advo-
> cates the destruction of the State of Israel), its overall
> strategy (the employment of terrorism and its consistent
> resistance to the peace process), the military infrastructure
> it constructed in the Gaza Strip, its radical Islamic nature,
> its use of force and occasional brutality in dealing with
> opponents (particularly Fatah), the process of enforced
> Islamization of the Gaza Strip, and the direction and sup-
> port it receives from its headquarters in Damascus. The
> Report does not refer to Hamas and other organizations in
> the Gaza Strip as terrorist organizations, in complete con-
> tradiction to not only the Israeli but also the American and
> European Union positions, all of which have designated

them, both their political and military wings, as terrorist organizations.[15]

It is no surprise then that the Goldstone report ignores or denies a host of related facts about Hamas crucial to the evaluation of the lawfulness of Israel's conduct in Operation Cast Lead. Among these are Hamas's systematic integration of its political administration and its armed forces; Hamas's massive military buildup following Israel's total evacuation from the Gaza Strip in 2005, including Hamas's substantial increase in the number, range, and destructive power of its rockets; and the funding and arming of Hamas by Syria and Iran.

While omitting vital facts, the Goldstone report uncritically accepts Hamas's narrative about the cause of the conflict and Hamas's version of specific events during Operation Cast Lead. Indeed, the Goldstone report goes so far as to assert that "In the framing of Israeli military objectives with regard to the Gaza operations, the concept of Hamas's 'supporting infrastructure' is particularly worrying as it appears to transform civilians and civilian objects into legitimate targets." That is a perverse inversion: As the ITIC study shows at great length and with massive supporting evidence, the unlawful transformation of civilians and civilian objects into supporting infrastructure for violent jihad against Israel was not a result of Israel's framing but rather an essential feature of Hamas's strategy.

---

15. "Hamas and the Terrorist Threat from the Gaza Strip: The Main Findings of the Goldstone Report Versus the Factual Findings," p. 3.

Israel's lengthy preliminary July 2009 statement on the factual and legal aspects of Operation Cast Lead, its January 2009 update, and the extensively documented March 2010 ITIC study on Hamas terrorism discredit the Goldstone report's factual and legal findings. But there is a larger and more fundamental problem. Under prevailing international law, the Goldstone mission lacked proper legal foundations.

Flawed Legal Foundations

The undertaking assigned to Goldstone and his colleagues by the United Nations Human Rights Council, the manner in which the Goldstone team carried out its mandate, and the UN General Assembly's endorsement of the Goldstone report contravened underlying norms and explicit provisions of existing international law.

The Goldstone mission, established on April 3, 2009, by the president of the Human Rights Council, was "to investigate all violations of international human rights law and international humanitarian law that might have been committed at any time in the context of the military operations that were conducted in Gaza during the period from 27 December 2008 and 18 January 2009, whether before, during or after."[16]

This mandate laid the foundations for an improper arrogation of power in two respects. First, it led to trampling, not only by the Goldstone report but also by the Human Rights Council and the General Assembly, on the primary responsibility assigned by the UN Charter to the Security

---

16. Goldstone report, Part I, Par. 131.

Council to deal with international peace and security. Second, and more importantly, it paved the way for the infringement by the Goldstone report, the HRC, and the General Assembly of the primary right and responsibility that multiple sources of international law accord to Israel, as a nation-state, to investigate, prosecute and, when proven, punish allegations of unlawful conduct against its armed forces.

Consider first how the General Assembly, by means of the Goldstone report and the HRC, subverted the division of powers established by the UN Charter between it and the Security Council. In Article 24, the UN Charter specifies that the Security Council has "primary responsibility for the maintenance of international peace and security." At the same time, the UN Charter reserves a limited role for the General Assembly in matters pertaining to international peace and security.

Article 10 gives it generally wide latitude to discuss and make recommendations while also highlighting a crucial limitation:

> The General Assembly may discuss any questions or any matters within the scope of the present Charter or relating to the powers and functions of any organs provided for in the present Charter, and, except as provided in Article 12, may make recommendations to the Members of the United Nations or to the Security Council or to both on any such questions or matter.

Article 12 states the limitation clearly:

> While the Security Council is exercising in respect of any dispute or situation the functions assigned to it in the

present Charter, the General Assembly shall not make any recommendation with regard to that dispute or situation unless the Security Council so requests.

On January 8, 2009, in the midst of Operation Cast Lead, the Security Council, consistent with Article 24 of the UN Charter, seized itself of the Gaza conflict. While continuing to be seized of it, the Security Council never asked the General Assembly for its recommendations. Yet the Goldstone report, authorized by the Human Rights Council and thus by its parent body, the General Assembly, not only presented factual findings and legal findings but also offered recommendations to the Security Council and to members of the United Nations. And both the HRC and the General Assembly endorsed those recommendations. In doing so, they directly contravened Article 12 of the UN Charter.

Not all actions undertaken by the General Assembly in connection to the Gaza conflict obviously contravened the UN Charter. For example, while the battle still raged, and after the Security Council seized itself of the conflict, the General Assembly seized itself of the matter, too. The full General Assembly urged the parties to heed Security Council resolution 1860 (the United States abstained), which called for ceasing of hostilities. Arguably, no interference with Security Council primacy occurred, because the General Assembly simply affirmed the Security Council's resolution.

The same cannot be said of the Human Rights Council's initial intervention, which also took place in the midst of the Gaza operation. Despite the absence of a request from the Security Council, the HRC—which as a creature of the General Assembly is, according to well-established principles of international law, bound by the same rules as its parent—made definite recommendations in Resolution S-9/1 (January 12, 2009).[17] Among other things, it "Call[ed] for the immediate cessation of Israeli military attacks"; "Demand[ed] that the occupying Power, Israel, immediately withdraw its military forces from the occupied Gaza Strip"; "Demand[ed] that the occupying Power, Israel, stop the targeting of civilians and medical facilities and staff and the systematic destruction of the cultural heritage of the Palestinian people"; and, not least, "Decide[d] to dispatch an urgent, independent international fact-finding mission, to be appointed by the President of the Council, to investigate all violations of international human rights law and international humanitarian law by the occupying Power, Israel, against the Palestinian people throughout the Occupied Palestinian Territory, particularly in the occupied Gaza Strip, due to the current aggression, and calls upon Israel not to obstruct the process of investigation and to fully cooperate with the mission."[18] All of the Human Rights Council's demands for action by, and against, Israel conflicted with Article 12 of the UN Charter.

---

17. Available at http://domino.un.org/unispal.nsf/0/404e93e16653 3f828525754e00559e30.

18. Mary Robinson, former president of Ireland and noted human rights champion, declined an early invitation to head such a Human Rights Council mission on the grounds that the HRC mandate referred only to violations by Israel and not also by Palestinians. See "Accounting for Gaza," available at http://www.theelders.org/article/ accounting-gaza. Justice Goldstone frequently points out that he successfully sought a mandate that also included instructions to investigate unlawful conduct by Palestinians. Yet the fundamental flaws in their report indicate that he and his colleagues carried out their investigation in the spirit of the original mandate.

Other conflicts followed. With its publication in September 2009, including ten pages of aggressive recommendations, the Goldstone report contravened Article 12. Among other things, it called for changes in Israeli policy in the West Bank, in East Jerusalem, and in the detention of Palestinians; urged the UN Secretary-General to submit the report to the Security Council; recommended that the Human Rights Council submit the report to the International Criminal Court (ICC); and advised states around the world to invoke universal jurisdiction to initiate criminal investigations against Israel in their domestic courts. In its report of October 21, 2009, the Human Rights Council disregarded Article 12 by endorsing the Goldstone report recommendations.[19] And in its Resolution 64/10 of December 1, 2009, the General Assembly disregarded Article 12 by endorsing the HRC's endorsement of the Goldstone report recommendations.[20]

Some contend that the report avoided trespassing on Security Council prerogatives by declining to address the legality of Israel's decision to undertake the Gaza operation (*jus ad bellum*) and instead dealing only with the legality of the conduct of the operation (*jus in bello*). But concerning the central legal question that arises in asymmetric warfare, the distinction is not sustainable. As the failings of the Goldstone report make abundantly clear, it is often impossible to properly assess the proportionality of any particular exercise of force in asymmetric warfare absent

---

19. Available at http://domino.un.org/unispal.nsf/0/93c22cea660f a96e85257657004cf8e6.

20. Available at http://domino.un.org/unispal.nsf/0/9cc062414581 d038852576c10055b066.

an understanding of the complex circumstances that initially justified the use of force.

Admittedly, the division of powers enshrined in the UN Charter does not appear to have had much impact in recent years on General Assembly practice. The General Assembly and its subsidiaries routinely make recommendations regarding matters of which the Security Council has declared itself seized but concerning which the Security Council has not requested General Assembly input. Accordingly, one might argue that the Security Council's failure to protest arrogation by the General Assembly and its subsidiaries of its prerogatives has diluted Article 12, or even rendered it a dead letter. Indeed, according to the International Court of Justice's (ICJ) advisory opinion "Legal Consequences of the Construction of a Wall in the Occupied Palestinian Territory" (2004), the "interpretation of Article 12 has evolved," and "the accepted practice of the General Assembly, as it has evolved, is consistent with Article 12, paragraph 1, of the Charter."[21] The ICJ opinion also notes, "It is often the case that, while the Security Council has tended to focus on the aspects of such matters related to international peace and security, the General Assembly has taken a broader view, considering also their humanitarian, social and economic aspects."

Even if the ICJ opinion were sound, it could not be fairly said that the Goldstone report restricted itself to the "humanitarian, social and economic" aspects of Israel's Gaza Operation. Indeed, its mandate directed it not only

---

21. Available at http://www.icj-cij.org/docket/files/131/1677.pdf.

"to investigate all violations of international human rights" but also all violations of "international humanitarian law," which governs conduct in war.

A further problem with this line of argument is that with a little ingenuity and a lot of brazenness virtually all of the conduct of war can be subsumed under its humanitarian, social, and economic aspects. This was illustrated by Miguel d'Escoto Brockmann, the president of the General Assembly's 63rd session, on January 15, 2009. In opening the 32nd Plenary Meeting of the 10th Emergency Special Session on the "Illegal Israeli Actions in Occupied East Jerusalem and the Rest of the Occupied Palestinian Territory," he contended that because Security Council resolution 1860 failed to address the humanitarian and economic crises brought about by the Gaza fighting and Israeli border restrictions it was incumbent upon the General Assembly to achieve a ceasefire and unimpeded humanitarian access.[22] Under such a theory, since in war civilians inevitably suffer unintended humanitarian, social, and economic harms the General Assembly will always have the prerogative to intervene in matters of international peace and security regardless of Security Council actions or requests.

To the extent that Security Council acquiescence to General Assembly usurpation has rendered Article 12 irrelevant, and the ICJ and the General Assembly have redefined war in terms of its humanitarian, social, and economic aspects, the Security Council's role as the international

---

22. Available at http://www.un.org/ga/president/63/statements/onpalestine150109.shtml.

body with "primary responsibility for the maintenance of international peace and security" has been significantly diminished. Indeed, these changes threaten to render the system of collective security established by the UN Charter entirely dysfunctional.

Even if the Human Rights Council and the General Assembly were not barred by the division of powers established by the UN Charter from making recommendations about the Gaza operation while the Security Council was seized of it and absent a Security Council request, the Goldstone report would still conflict with the requirements of international law. The second, and more weighty, set of conflicts flows out of a principle of deference to national courts that is inscribed in a variety of authoritative international law sources. According to this principle, it is, in the first instance, the right and the responsibility of nation-states themselves to carry out investigations concerning allegations of war crimes and to prosecute and punish where warranted. Of course deference is not a blank check: national courts can be found disinclined or incompetent to carry out their responsibilities under international law. Nevertheless, the principle of deference—rooted in the United Nations Charter, the Geneva Conventions, customary international law, and the statute governing the ICC—creates a substantial protected sphere for the operation of domestic legal systems. The Goldstone mission contravened the principle of deference.

Article 2 of the UN Charter declares:

Nothing contained in the present Charter shall authorize the United Nations to intervene in matters which are essentially within the domestic jurisdiction of any state or shall require the Members to submit such matters to settlement under the present Charter; but this principle shall not prejudice the application of enforcement measures under Chapter VII.

One of the critical matters that international law places within the domestic jurisdiction of states is primary responsibility for the investigation and prosecution of war crimes.

Article 146 of the Fourth Geneva Convention is a key legal source for this right and responsibility:

> The High Contracting Parties undertake to enact any legislation necessary to provide effective penal sanctions for persons committing, or ordering to be committed, any of the grave breaches of the present Convention defined in the following Article.
>
> Each High Contracting Party shall be under the obligation to search for persons alleged to have committed, or to have ordered to be committed, such grave breaches, and shall bring such persons, regardless of their nationality, before its own courts. It may also, if it prefers, and in accordance with the provisions of its own legislation, hand such persons over for trial to another High Contracting Party concerned, provided such High Contracting Party has made out a prima facie case.
>
> Each High Contracting Party shall take measures necessary for the suppression of all acts contrary to the provisions of the present Convention other than the grave breaches defined in the following Article.

In all circumstances, the accused persons shall benefit
by safeguards of proper trial and defense, which shall not
be less favourable than those provided by Article 105 and
those following of the Geneva Convention relative to the
Treatment of Prisoners of War of 12 August 1949.[23]

To be sure, Article 146 articulates a general obligation
binding on all High Contracting Parties, not just on parties to a conflict. But it was understood at the time of the
drafting and has been recognized in foreign relations law
since that priority goes to the states accused and the states
aggrieved.

This understanding comports with the International
Committee of the Red Cross (ICRC) commentary on
Article 146:

The obligation on the High Contracting Parties to search
for persons accused to have committed grave breaches
imposes an active duty on them. As soon as a Contracting
Party realizes that there is on its territory a person who has
committed such a breach, its duty is to ensure that the person concerned is arrested and prosecuted with all speed.
The necessary police action should be taken spontane-
ously, therefore, not merely in pursuance of a request from
another State. The court proceedings should be carried
out in a uniform manner whatever the nationality of the
accused. Nationals, friends, enemies, all should be subject
to the same rules of procedure and judged by the same

---

23. Available at http://www.icrc.org/ihl.nsf/9ac284404d38ed2bc
1256311002afd89/6f96ee4c7d1e72cac12563cd0051c63a.

courts. There is therefore no question of setting up special tribunals to try war criminals of enemy nationality.[24]

States' active duty to search for war crimes perpetrators on their territory confirms the special role that accused and aggrieved states have under Article 146 to launch investigations, pursue suspects, make arrests, undertake prosecutions, and impose punishments.

Yet in the Gaza conflict, the General Assembly and its subsidiary, the Human Rights Council, showed no deference to Israel's right and responsibility to deal with war crimes accusations. Indeed, by prematurely authorizing an investigation even before the guns fell silent in Gaza, the Human Rights Council cast dark aspersions on Israel's system of military justice and civilian oversight. And then well before Israel could reasonably have completed preliminary investigations of war crimes allegations, let alone initiated criminal trials, the Goldstone report produced factual and legal findings, swiftly endorsed by the Human Rights Council and the General Assembly, that convicted IDF commanders and soldiers of war crimes and crimes against humanity in the court of international public opinion. This struck at the independence of Israel's judicial system and interfered with its ability to discharge its Article 146 active duty.

Furthermore, the Goldstone report's recommendation that the Security Council refer Israel to the International Criminal Court in the event that Israel did not comply with

---

24. See the ICRC commentary "Convention (IV) relative to the Protection of Civilian Persons in Time of War. Geneva, 12 August 1949," available at http://www.icrc.org/ihl.nsf/COM/380-600168.

the report's specific demands showed a misunderstanding of the ICC's function. That misunderstanding is of special interest because it revolves around the very principle of deference to national courts over which the Goldstone report rides roughshod.

The Rome Statute, which established the ICC, confirms the primacy that international law assigns to states to handle war crimes accusations. Article 17 lays out an expression of the principle of deference that has come to be called the "complementarity principle." It provides that a condition for the admissibility of a case is that "the State is unwilling or unable genuinely to carry out the investigation or prosecution."[25] The principle of deference is also built into the tight limitations on the crimes that the ICC is authorized to handle. The ICC does not exist to prosecute every crime that happens in wartime. It is reserved only for the most heinous and enormous, the kind of crimes, that is, whose very commission implies that state courts are unable or unwilling to investigate and prosecute.

In a February 2006 letter explaining his decision to decline the many requests to investigate war crimes allegations against coalition troops in Iraq, ICC prosecutor Luis Moreno-Ocampo stressed that the scale of the alleged crimes was critical.[26] Under the Rome Statute, initiation of an ICC investigation requires that a case must meet both a specific and general gravity standard. The specific standard

---

25. Available at http://untreaty.un.org/cod/icc/statute/99_corr/2.htm.
26. Available at http://www.icc-cpi.int/NR/rdonlyres/F596D08D-D810-43A2-99BB-B899B9C5BCD2/277422/OTP_letter_to_senders_re_Iraq_9_February_2006.pdf.

involves crimes committed "as part of a plan or policy or as part of a large-scale commission of such crimes." The general standard requires that the crime itself be of surpassing magnitude. Ocampo found no evidence that the alleged crimes committed by coalition forces in Iraq were part of any plan or policy, so they failed to meet the specific gravity standard. He further observed that the cases the ICC had accepted involved the willful killing of hundreds of thousands of people, large-scale sexual violence and abductions, and the displacement of millions. The alleged misconduct in Iraq did not belong in anything like the same class: "The number of potential victims of crimes within the jurisdiction of the Court in this situation— 4 to 12 victims of willful killing and a limited number of victims of inhuman treatment—was of a different order than the number of victims found in other situations under investigation or analysis by the Office." Thus the criminal allegations concerning coalition forces in Iraq didn't meet the general gravity standard either. Therefore, Ocampo concluded, the charges were inadmissible for investigation and prosecution by the ICC.

Like the principle of complementarity, the gravity standard reflects the primacy international law attaches to the right and responsibility of states to investigate and prosecute war crimes. It does this by creating an exceedingly high hurdle for ICC intervention. The case that the Goldstone report makes against Israel does not come close to clearing it. The report does accuse Israel of deliberately seeking to terrorize the Palestinian population, which, notwithstanding Goldstone's retraction, might meet the specific gravity standard for admissibility. However, and setting aside the Goldstone report's grave defects, its accusations against

Israel would still not have met the ICC's general gravity standard. What is decisive is that while the number of civilian deaths for which the Goldstone report found Israel responsible was considerably larger—in the hundreds—than the number involved in the complaints against coalition forces in Iraq, the number of deaths was nevertheless of a substantially lesser order than those, as Ocampo explained in his letter on military operations in Iraq, that are necessary to meet the ICC's general gravity standard.

Because the allegations against Israel failed to meet the ICC's general gravity standard, the Goldstone report's recommendation that the Security Council refer the matter to the ICC was without merit. In pressing those recommendations, the report not only displayed an ignorance of, or indifference to, the law under which the ICC operates. It also, and again, demonstrated its obliviousness to the right and responsibility of states, in the first instance, to deal with war crimes accusations.

Ocampo's reasoning in his Iraq letter about the narrow limits within which the ICC was designed to operate is in line with his general views about the presumption in international law that states are the appropriate initial authority for handling most war crimes investigations and prosecutions. In his statement at his swearing in on June 16, 2003, he emphasized the principle of deference to national courts:

> The Court is complementary to national systems. This means that whenever there is genuine State action, the Court cannot and will not intervene.
>
> But States not only have the right, but also the primary responsibility to prevent, control and prosecute atrocities.

Complementarity protects national sovereignty and at the same time promotes state action.

The effectiveness of the International Criminal Court should not be measured by the number of cases that reach it. On the contrary, complementarity implies that the absence of trials before this Court, as a consequence of the regular functioning of national institutions, would be a major success.

For this reason, the first task of the Office of the Prosecutor will be to establish links with prosecutors and judges from all over the world.

They continue to bear primary responsibility for investigating and prosecuting the crimes within the jurisdiction of the Court, and we are confident that they will make every effort to carry out their duties.

We wish to interact with them in order to establish a network of national and international prosecutors who will co-operate with each other and develop the ability to function together.[27]

One could hardly wish for a clearer statement from a better-positioned official affirming the primacy that international law accords to states to investigate and prosecute accusations against their citizens of unlawful conduct in war. By failing to appreciate this primacy, the Goldstone mission infringed on Israel's rights, interfered with its responsibilities, and violated fundamental norms and principles of international law.

---

27. Available at http://www.iccnow.org/documents/MorenoOcampo 16June03.pdf.

The only relevant cases where international authorities were given the power to preempt local prosecutions were the ad hoc tribunals established for the former Yugoslavia (1993) and Rwanda (1994) in the midst of internal conflict and civic breakdown in which the normal presumption in favor of domestic accountability may appear to have been reversed. But those tribunals, for which Justice Goldstone served as prosecutor, are better seen as clarifying the limits to the deference international law grants to national courts. The International Criminal Tribunal for the former Yugoslavia (ICTY) and the International Criminal Tribunal for Rwanda (ICTR) dealt with situations in which civil war and massive killing either overwhelmed the ability or demonstrated the unwillingness of national governments to undertake the impartial, independent, and diligent investigations and prosecutions of war crimes required by international law. But in contrast to war-torn former Yugoslavia and genocide-ravaged Rwanda, Israel possesses a judicial system, as any impartial and objective review would show, that is on a par with the most admired judicial systems in the world.

It does not follow that international institutions were obliged to sit on the sidelines until Israel had completed its investigations and prosecutions arising out of Operation Cast Lead. For example, the ICRC's contribution respected Israel's rights and responsibilities as a sovereign state. In the summer of 2009, the ICRC submitted a confidential report to the government of Israel; it involved no recommendations to other international bodies and neither sought nor had any impact on international public opinion. It was intended only to provide information to enable Israel to better carry out its active duty under international law to investigate and prosecute war crimes connected to the Gaza operation.

Had it proceeded in the spirit of the ICRC, the Human Rights Council too might have played a lawful and constructive role in the months following the conclusion of the Gaza conflict. It might, for example, have appointed a task force to review the complex and multilayered judicial system that Israel has established for the investigation and prosecution of war crimes. A competent and lawful review might have involved submission of a confidential report to Israel that identified where the country's judicial system could be improved to comport with international standards as reflected in best practices around the world—in contrast to the Goldstone report's condemnation of Israel for failing to live up to an idealized system of international criminal justice. This would have respected Israel's rights, and aided Israel in complying with its responsibilities, under international law.

How little the majority of members of the Human Rights Council actually care about the impartial and objective application of international law and the protection of human rights was shown in May 2009, less than two months after the HRC authorized the Goldstone mission. Sri Lanka had just defeated the Tamil Tigers in their twenty-five-year war. UN officials estimated that in its advance into the Tamil north the Sri Lankan army killed more than 10,000 civilians, with some estimates at the time going as high as 20,000 and current estimates reaching 30,000. Credible reports indicated that government forces herded civilians into a "no fire" zone in the north and then shelled it. Cell phone video, which the top UN envoy in Sri Lanka considered genuine, showed government forces executing naked and bound captives. The government was directly linked to hundreds of disappearances, and held approximately 300,000 civilians in poor conditions in detention camps. Nevertheless, the Human Rights Council rejected a draft resolution that deplored the actions of both sides, and which called for an independent investigation. Instead, on May 28, 2009, as Goldstone and his team were proceeding with their work, the Human Rights Council passed resolution S-11/1, which "reaffirm[ed]" the UN Charter's "principle of non-interference in matters that are essentially within the domestic jurisdiction of States."[28] The only condemnation the resolution offered was directed at the defeated Tamil Tigers. The Sri Lankan government received nothing but encouragement from the Human Rights Council for its conduct. Eight months later, in January of 2010, after reelection as president of Sri Lanka (amid low turnout among Tamils, and reported voter intimidation and violence in Tamil regions), Mahinda Rajapaksa declared that his victory proved that his government had committed no war crimes, and that no investigation, internal or otherwise, was needed. The United Nations Human Rights Council could see no reason to disagree.[29]

---

28. Available at http://www2.ohchr.org/english/bodies/hrcouncil/docs/11specialsession/S-11-1-Final-E.doc.

29. On June 3, 2010—more than a year after the HRC had formally pronounced its satisfaction with Sri Lanka's conduct—Philip Alston, special rapporteur on extrajudicial, summary, or arbitrary executions for the HRC, in presenting his annual report, called for an "independent international inquiry" into "allegations that as many as 30,000 persons were killed in Sri Lanka in the closing months of the conflict and that grave violations of human rights and humanitarian law were committed." At the same time, Alston called for an "independent international inquiry" into Israel's "attack on the humanitarian

Who Judges?

The United Nations Human Rights Council is a travesty. A majority of its members appear to take a cynical view of international law, conceiving of it as a tool for punishing enemies and rewarding friends, and regarding Israel as the most odious of enemies and the principal threat to international order.

But it would be a mistake to conclude from the HRC's enmity toward Israel and the Goldstone report's flawed legal foundations that the western international human rights lawyers, professors of law, and intellectuals who have uncritically championed the Goldstone report's findings and endorsed its recommendations also subscribe to a cynical view of international law. On the contrary, many Goldstone report supporters are animated by an idealized understanding of international law according to which it crystallizes humanity's considered judgments about morality and war, and an idealized understanding of international institutions according to which the men and women who operate them embody a form of transnational or global governance that operates above the fray of nation-state power politics. To advance the cause of international peace and global justice, they maintain, critical judgments about the lawful conduct of war—including the crucial question in asymmetric warfare of what constitutes a proportional use of force—should be taken out of the hands of nation-states and placed in those of international institutions.

---

flotilla off Gaza," an attack that occurred only days before and in which Israeli commandos, in self defense, killed nine militants who were part of a mission to break Israel's lawful maritime blockade of Gaza.

These men and women are blinded to the Goldstone report's grave flaws by the higher cause they believe it serves. Indeed, the scandal of the Goldstone report—which includes both its grave flaws and the blindness to them of many practitioners of international law—gives good reason, certainly for liberal democracies with well-developed judicial systems, to preserve the right and primary responsibility of states, inscribed in authoritative sources of international law, to adjudicate the difficult questions that arise under the international laws of war.

The worthy ambition to hold perpetrators accountable for unlawful conduct in war must not be allowed to obscure the obstacles to designing international institutions capable of impartially and objectively crafting, adjudicating, and enforcing the international laws of war. These obstacles include the emergence of a transnational elite with interests and ambitions of its own; the lack among this elite of democratic accountability and national security responsibility; the domination of the General Assembly by authoritarian states; and the absence in many cases of agreed upon authority for adjudicating and enforcing the international laws of war. Until these obstacles are overcome—and we are a long way off—justice will be better served by preserving the right and primary responsibility of states to vindicate, through their own judicial systems, the international laws of war, especially when those states are established liberal democracies. International institutions should be reserved, consistent with the principle of deference, as a judicial system of last resort.

The revolution in international law that the Goldstone report seeks to advance affects directly only a small number of countries, all of which are liberal democracies. Russia, China, Iran, and the host of lesser authoritarian regimes around the globe rarely pay more than lip service to human rights and to their obligations under the international laws of war. Transnational terrorists openly scoff at, even as they determinedly manipulate, such rights and obligations. Meanwhile, most of the world's liberal democracies, whose commitments to individual freedom and human equality inculcate respect for human rights and the principles that undergird the international laws of war, seldom take up arms. Among liberal democracies, Israel and the United States in particular depend daily on their armed forces to protect their way of life. And paradoxically, while no armies in the history of warfare have devoted greater attention than those of Israel and the United States to distinguishing and protecting civilians in warfare and ensuring that the force they use in armed conflict is proportional to the threat faced, no armies today come under greater worldwide attack for violating the laws of war and human rights than those of Israel and the United States.

Although Israel and the United States confront a common enemy, their strategic situations differ dramatically. Israel is tiny and faces adversaries—to the immediate north in southern Lebanon, Iran-sponsored Hezbollah; to the immediate southwest in Gaza and immediate east in the West Bank, Iran-sponsored Hamas; and a thousand miles to the east, but within Shahab-3 ballistic missile range, the Islamic Republic of Iran itself—that seek its destruction through violent jihad. To the immediate northeast, Israel also confronts Iran-sponsored Syria, which is armed to the teeth and provides an overland route for the supply of arms to Hezbollah in Lebanon. Accordingly, Israel maintains the region's most powerful conventional military and a nuclear deterrent.

Meanwhile, the United States remains the world's sole superpower and the only nation capable of promptly and decisively projecting force anywhere in the world. It is surrounded by friendly neighbors and vast oceans while shouldering responsibility for keeping open the world's sea lanes, ensuring safety in the skies, and generally serving as the international political and economic order's chief law enforcement officer. At the same time, the United States remains engaged in a protracted transnational struggle with the same forces of Islamic extremism that menace Israel.

Despite their common enemy, Israel and the United States stand in different relationships to the project, of which the Goldstone report is one initiative, to expand the authority of international institutions to take primary responsibility for critical judgments about the lawful conduct of war. It is obviously in Israel's interest to oppose such a transfer of power to international bodies, which are stacked against it. And while Washington has provided indispensable support over the decades for Israel's security interests, it is easy to understand why the United States, whose wealth, power, and Security Council veto insulate it from the machinations of the General Assembly and its subsidiary organs, might wish to downplay the matter.

But that is shortsighted. The danger is that the spread of practices among international bodies and an accumulation of precedents concerning international law will weigh down the United States in the struggle that it shares with Israel and all civilized nations to combat, in accordance with the international laws of war, transnational terrorism. Of course that will only happen if the United States recognizes such practices and precedents as authoritative.

Encouragement to do so comes from powerful trends in American universities, in political science departments and law schools. There, for going on a generation, professors have been cultivating in their students the view, which animates the Goldstone report but which conflicts with the international laws of war, that critical judgments about the lawful conduct of war are indeed properly and in the first instance the province of international institutions.

That view is suited to a world in which all nation-states incline to peace and govern themselves in accordance with liberal and democratic principles. Unfortunately, that is not the world in which we live. Nor is it a world we should expect will emerge anytime soon.

CHAPTER THREE

The Gaza Flotilla

On May 31, 2010, in defense of a naval blockade imposed on the Gaza Strip, Israel seized control of the *Mavi Marmara* in international waters, detained the passengers, and towed the ship to the Israeli port city of Ashdod. During the previous three days, and meeting only light resistance, Israel had boarded, inspected, and brought to Ashdod the other five ships that had set sail from Turkey as part of the "Gaza Freedom Flotilla." But on the *Mavi Marmara*, passengers wielding pipes, knives, and axes attacked Israeli commandos as they rappelled from helicopters down to the ship's deck. Nine passengers were killed in the operation and several dozen were injured. Seven commandos were injured as well.

The flotilla's ostensible purpose was to bring humanitarian goods to the Palestinian population of Gaza. In fact, humanitarian goods had been arriving in Gaza over land through Israel, and Israel had repeatedly volunteered to deliver the flotilla's humanitarian cargo through the established land crossings. The flotilla's real and obvious goal was, as stated by Greta Berlin, one of the organizers, "breaking Israel's siege."[1]

The international outcry in response to Israel's raid on the *Mavi Marmara* was immediate. Little attention was given to the Turkish flotilla's deliberate provocation or to the possibility that Israel had acted imprudently or ineptly. The focus rather was on the accusation, sometimes couched as a conclusion, that Israel had wantonly broken international law and was answerable to the world.

On May 31, almost as soon as the news broke, UN Secretary-General Ban Ki-moon demanded an accounting: "I condemn this violence . . . it is vital that there is a full investigation to determine exactly how this bloodshed took place . . . I believe Israel must urgently provide a full explanation."[2]

Richard Falk, UN Special Rapporteur on the Situation of Human Rights in the Occupied Palestinian Territory, issued his verdict in advance of investigation. He declared on May 31 that "Israel is guilty of shocking behavior by using deadly weapons against unarmed civilians on ships that were situated in the high seas where freedom of navigation exists, according to the law of the seas." Falk did call for an investigation, though not to determine wrongdoing but rather to place an official stamp on Israel's guilt: "It is essential that those Israelis responsible for this lawless and murderous behavior, including political leaders

---

1. "Tensions rise over Gaza aid fleet," *Al Jazeera*, May 28, 2010, available at http://www.aljazeera.com/news/middleeast/2010/05/2010528431964325.html.

2. BBC, May 31, 2011, available at http://www.bbc.co.uk/news/10196351.

who issued the orders, be held criminally accountable for their wrongful acts." He characterized the Gaza blockade as "a massive form of collective punishment" constituting "a crime against humanity, as well as a gross violation of the prohibition on collective punishment in Article 33 of the Fourth Geneva Convention." He insisted that failure to punish Israel's lawlessness would itself be criminal: "As Special Rapporteur for the Occupied Palestinian Territories, familiar with the suffering of the people of Gaza, I find this latest instance of Israeli military lawlessness to create a situation of regional and global emergency. Unless prompt and decisive action is taken to challenge the Israeli approach to Gaza all of us will be complicit in criminal policies that are challenging the survival of an entire beleaguered community." Such was Israel's "flagrant flouting of international law" that, to end its blockade of Gaza, Falk concluded, "the worldwide campaign of boycott, divestment, and sanctions against Israel is now a moral and political imperative, and needs to be supported and strengthened everywhere."[3]

Many nations promptly condemned Israel and some publicly proclaimed Israel's conduct unlawful. According to the BBC, within hours of the boarding of the *Mavi Marmara* French Foreign Minister Bernard Kouchner announced he was "deeply shocked" by Israel's action and called for an inquiry, and French President Nicolas Sarkozy accused Israel of a "disproportionate use of force." Sweden summoned the Israeli ambassador to discuss the "unacceptable

---

3. United Nations Office of the High Commissioner for Human Rights, May 31, 2010, available at http://www.ohchr.org/en/News Events/Pages/DisplayNews.aspx?NewsID=10080&LangID=E.

action." The Turkish foreign ministry issued a statement declaring the incident a "flagrant breach of international law" while Turkish Prime Minister Recep Tayyip Erdogan proclaimed Israel's raid "totally contrary to the principles of international law" and an act of "inhumane state terrorism." And the Arab League called for an emergency meeting the next day to discuss Israel's "terrorist act."[4]

On June 1, the UN Security Council issued a presidential statement. By condemning Israel's raid and by demanding a "prompt, impartial, credible, and transparent investigation conforming to international standards," the Security Council intervention indicated that there was sufficient evidence to believe that serious breaches of international law had occurred.[5]

Not to be outdone, on June 2 the notorious UN Human Rights Council (HRC) issued resolution 14/1 on "The Grave Attacks by Israeli Forces against the Humanitarian Boat Convoy."[6] The HRC resolution "condemns in the

---

4. The BBC timeline of events, "As it happened: Israeli raid on Gaza flotilla," is available at http://www.bbc.co.uk/news/10196585.

5. S/PRST/201019, available at http://www.un.org/News/Press/docs/20101sc9940.doc.htm.

6. Available at http://domino.un.org/unispal.nsf/0/4d2f5b28bb470a8e8525773d0051f543?. In favor (32): Angola, Argentina, Bahrain, Bangladesh, Bolivia, Bosnia and Herzegovina, Brazil, Chile, China, Cuba, Djibouti, Egypt, Gabon, Ghana, India, Indonesia, Jordan, Kyrgyzstan, Mauritius, Mexico, Nicaragua, Nigeria, Norway, Pakistan, Philippines, Qatar, Russian Federation, Saudi Arabia, Senegal, Slovenia, South Africa, and Uruguay. Against (3): Italy, Netherlands, and United States of America. Abstentions (9): Belgium, Burkina Faso, France, Hungary, Japan, Republic of Korea, Slovakia, Ukraine, and United Kingdom. Vote count and discussion available at http://unispal.un.org/unispal.nsf/0/64C49CB9EFCA5BAB852577360055ADE6.

strongest terms the outrageous attack by the Israeli forces against the humanitarian flotilla of ships which resulted in the killing and injuring of many innocent civilians from different countries." And it called for "an independent, international fact-finding mission to investigate violations of international law, including international humanitarian and human rights law, resulting from the Israeli attacks on the flotilla of ships carrying humanitarian assistance."

The widespread accusations of unlawful conduct directed at Israel—coming, it should be said, not from some abstract international community, but from officers and official bodies of the United Nations, European states, Turkey, and Arab states—were high on outrage and low on legal analysis. This was in keeping with the growing tendency in international affairs to transform hard political questions into conclusive legal judgments. The transformation increasingly yields glaring abuses of law. These abuses harm not only states involved in specific controversies but the interests of all civilized states in international laws of war that reasonably balance military necessity and humanitarian responsibility. Because of the rise of law as a universal language of international politics, even far-fetched and perverse legal arguments that gain currency must be addressed and refuted in legal terms.

The legality of Israel's stopping and seizing of the *Mavi Marmara* and the other five ships of the Gaza Freedom Flotilla hinged on the legality under the international laws of war of the naval blockade. If the blockade was legal, then Israel was perfectly within its rights to stop in international waters ships whose announced intention was to break it, and Israeli commandos were within their rights to defend themselves against the potentially lethal attacks to which they were subject as they boarded the *Mavi Marmara*.

Israel's blockade was legal given the state of armed conflict between Israel and Hamas, the de facto ruling authority of Gaza; the widely accepted use of naval blockades in war; and the conformity of Israel's blockade to the requirements of maritime law—it was duly declared, effective, nondiscriminatory, and allowed the passage of humanitarian assistance to the civilian population of Gaza. This was the key conclusion reached by both the Turkel Commission report,[7] authorized by the Israeli government to investigate the Gaza flotilla controversy, and the United Nations' "Report of the Secretary-General's Panel of Inquiry on the 31 May 2010 Flotilla Incident," commonly referred to as the Palmer report.[8]

---

7. Turkel report, Part I, p. 111, available at http://www.turkel -committee.gov.il/content-107.html.

8. Palmer report, available at http://www.un.org/News/dh/infocus/ middle_east/Gaza_Flotilla_Panel_Report.pdf, with conclusions about the lawfulness of the blockade discussed predominantly on pp. 38–45. The Palmer report is inherently more credible than the Goldstone report. Whereas the Palmer report examined Israel's reasoning as set forth in the Turkel report, the Goldstone report delivered one-sided condemnations, while disregarding Israel's interim report ("The Operation in Gaza: Factual and Legal Aspects," July 29, 2009, available at http://www.mfa.gov.il/NR/rdonlyres/E89E699D-A435-491B-B2D0-017675DAFEF7/0/GazaOperation.pdf) and proceeding with publication well before Israel could complete its investigations. By relying on the full reports submitted by Israel as well as Turkey, the Palmer report respected international law's emphasis on states' primary role in investigating war crimes allegations. And the Palmer report came out of the Secretary-General's office instead of the anti-Israel Human Rights Council. For the critique of the Goldstone report, see Chapter 2. For a more detailed exploration of the differences in origin, mandate and methodology between the two UN reports, see

Many, however, continue to cling to the contention that the blockade is illegal. According to the standard argument, the blockade violates international law because Israel continues to be an occupying power, and as such is barred from undertaking acts of war, such as a naval blockade, against Gaza. This argument is advanced notwithstanding Israel's disengagement from Gaza in the summer of 2005, in which Israel withdrew every soldier and every civilian, and despite the absence of any Israeli soldiers (except for Gilad Shalit, who was held by Hamas from June 2006 until October 2011 under conditions that violated the international laws of war) or citizens in Gaza on May 31, 2010, when the *Mavi Marmara* was seized.

The standard argument, however, is at best unpersuasive and is generally groundless and incoherent. It twists well-settled concepts, distorts basic categories, overlooks or obscures crucial facts, misreads critical cases, and ignores or misconstrues fundamental legal principles. Since Israel neither has troops stationed in Gaza nor exercises the functions of government there, it does not exercise "effective control" of Gaza, and therefore does not meet the test that the international laws of war establish to determine whether a territory is occupied by a hostile power.

More importantly, the argument over whether Israel occupies Gaza is ultimately irrelevant to determining the legality of its naval blockade. Even if Israel were deemed the occupying power, it would not lose its inherent right of

"Palmer vs. Goldstone: Lessons Learned," by Gerald M. Steinberg and Gidon Shaviv, in the *Jerusalem Post*, Sept. 7, 2011, available at http://www.jpost.com/Opinion/Op-EdContributors/Article .aspx?id=237095.

self-defense, recognized by the UN Charter and the international laws of war, to repel Hamas's acts of aggression. Indeed, since it seized complete control of Gaza in June 2007, Hamas's public declarations, bombardment of Israeli civilian populations, unremitting efforts to conduct terrorist operations against Israel, and, after Israel's December 2008–January 2009 Gaza operation, its rearmament in preparation for the renewal of rocket and missile attacks, have placed it in a condition of war with Israel. Accordingly, Israel is entitled under the international laws of war to impose a naval blockade of Gaza to prevent Hamas from acquiring additional weapons of war. Of course, Israel remains obliged to permit civilian humanitarian requirements to be met.

The widespread opinion that the Israeli blockade of Gaza is illegal and the shabby reasoning that underwrites it threaten the integrity of the international laws of war. As in the case of the Goldstone report before it, in the case of the Gaza flotilla influential international public opinion has coalesced around a view of the international laws of war that substitutes propaganda for credible legal analysis. As with the Goldstone report controversy, so too with the Gaza flotilla controversy: exposing the abuses to which the international laws of war have been subject and setting forth a sounder view is critical to conserving them. And conserving the international laws of war is a task in which all nations devoted to the rule of law have a stake—liberal democracies in particular, and especially liberal democracies such as the United States that are actively engaged in armed struggle against transnational terrorists. And, as with the Goldstone report, so too with the Gaza flotilla controversy: that task requires a critique of the majority view; a restatement of longstanding principles of the international laws of war; and, above all, a recovery of the imperative to strike a reasonable balance between military necessity and humanitarian responsibility, the imperative out of which the international laws of war emerged and which must remain its governing goal.

The Occupation Argument

To vindicate the standard argument that Israel is prohibited from maintaining a naval blockade of Gaza because it is an occupying power, it is necessary to overcome the well-settled definition of occupation and the established test for determining whether an occupation has come into existence.

The law of occupation is rooted in two principal provisions of the international laws of war. According to Article 42 of the 1907 Hague Regulations, "territory is considered occupied when it is actually placed under the authority of the hostile army. The occupation extends only to the territory where such authority has been established and can be exercised."[9] And Article 6 of the Fourth Geneva Convention provides that a state achieves established authority and becomes an occupying power in a territory "to the extent that such Power exercises the functions of government in such territory."[10]

The legal test is whether the hostile army has placed territory and its population under "effective control." On the basis of an extensive review of the legal materials, Elizabeth Sampson observes that "'effective control' is a term of art

---

9. Available at http://www.icrc.org /ihl.nsf/full/195.
10. Available at http://www.icrc.org/ihl.nsf/webart/380-600009.

with no definite source, but it has developed as the standard that combines the conditions for occupation outlined in the Hague Regulations and the Fourth Geneva Convention."[11] Case law and state practice, moreover, indicate general agreement that to exercise effective control in the legally relevant sense is to perform the functions of government, which typically requires troops in the territory.

Israel in Gaza obviously does not meet the test, at least as commonly understood. Israel has not had troops stationed in Gaza, or indeed any permanent presence there, military or civilian, since September 2005, when it completed the disengagement process it began the month before. When Israel left Gaza, the Palestinian Authority (PA) took over the functions of government. Following Hamas's victory in the January 2006 Palestinian Legislative Council elections, the PA continued to govern in Gaza until June 2007, when Hamas violently overthrew it and took complete control. Since then, Hamas has exercised the functions of government in Gaza. In early January 2009, shortly after the beginning of Operation Cast Lead, Israel imposed a naval blockade, the primary purpose of which was to prevent the arrival into Gaza of weapons and other military supplies. At the conclusion of the operation, Israel brought home all troops but maintained the blockade.

Nevertheless, influential segments of international public opinion and international legal opinion insist that Israel occupies Gaza. The routine characterization of Gaza as occupied—in, among other places, UN Human Rights

---

11. Elizabeth Sampson, "Is Gaza Occupied? Redefining the Legal Status of Gaza," *Mideast Security and Policy Studies* 83, available at http://www.biu.ac.il/Besa/MSPS83.pdf.

Council, General Assembly, and Security Council resolutions[12]—is backed by a set of oft-repeated legal arguments.

Among the leading advocates of the standard argument is Noura Erakat, adjunct professor of international human rights law in the Middle East at Georgetown University and the US-based legal advocacy coordinator for Badil Resource Center for Palestinian Residency and Refugee Rights. To maintain that since its complete withdrawal from Gaza in 2005 Israel has occupied Gaza, Erakat reinterprets the meaning of "effective control." Crucial to her position is rejection of the view that a hostile military presence throughout the territory is required by the "effective control" test. Rather, she points to decisions by the Nuremberg Tribunal and the International Criminal Tribunal for the former Yugoslavia that, according to her, consider an occupation ongoing where there is "the capacity to send troops within a reasonable time to make the authority of the occupying power felt."[13] Israel retains this capacity, Erakat contends, and, through repeated military operations since the Gaza disengagement, has demonstrated its willingness to use it.

In practice, according to Erakat, Israel exercises control over the Palestinians of Gaza in a variety of ways. Because it controls entrance into and exit from Gaza, including

---

12. UN Security Council Resolution 1860 (2009). Also, from the session that began in September 2010, General Assembly Resolutions 65/102, 65/103, 65/104, 65/105, 65/179, available at http://www.un.org/en/ga/65/resolutions.shtml.

13. Noura Erakat, "It's Not Wrong, It's Illegal: Situating the Gaza Blockade Between International Law and the UN Response" (2010), p. 11, available at http://www.law.utoronto.ca/documents/ihrp/Noura Erakatarticle.pdf.

control of land crossings and all air and sea access to Gaza, Israel determines the flow of people and goods in and out of Gaza. Israel controls Gaza's electricity supply, and so possesses the power to turn its lights on and off. Israel's restrictions on the entry into Gaza of "dual-use" goods—that is, goods that can be used for military as well as civilian purposes—has created a shortage of spare parts to maintain wastewater treatment plants and construct buildings. Furthermore, Israel retains control over some of Gaza's telecommunications networks, its electromagnetic sphere, its fuel supply, its population registry, and the collection and distribution of a substantial amount of Palestinian tax revenue.

Among proponents of the standard argument, some of whom are Israeli, it is commonly asserted that the primary purpose of the control Israel exercises, or its closure policy, is not to maintain security but to exert pressure.[14] Even Israel's Turkel Commission report grants that the blockade is also intended as "indirect economic warfare" to put political pressure on Hamas.[15] Many opponents of the blockade allege that Israel has used disproportionate force by depriving an entire civilian population of sufficient quantities of basic goods because a few militants have been firing relatively ineffectual rockets.[16] Furthermore, Erakat argues,

---

14. "Gaza Closure Defined: Collective Punishment," available at http://gisha.org/UserFiles/File/publications/GazaClosureDefined Eng.pdf.

15. Turkel report, pp. 56–58, 71.

16. Victor Kattan, "Operation Cast Lead: Use of Force Discourses and Jus Ad Bellum Controversies," *The Palestine Handbook of International Law* (2009), available at http://www.victorkattan.com/cms Admin/uploads/Victor_Kattan_BRILL.pdf.

Israeli troops might as well be stationed in Gaza inasmuch as in its disengagement plan "Israel reserved the right to use force against Palestinians living in Gaza in the name of preventive and reactive self-defense."[17]

What the various forms of control Israel exercises over Gaza add up to, concludes Erakat, is clear: "The confluence of its ongoing control, its continuous military operations, as well as its capacity to redeploy its troops within a reasonable time demonstrate that Israel remains in effective control of the Gaza Strip."[18] Therefore, despite lacking troops on the ground and not exercising the functions of government in Gaza, Israel should be seen under international humanitarian law as occupying Gaza.

Accordingly, the standard argument continues, Israel is barred by international law from taking military action—attacks, blockades, or otherwise—against Gaza. In particular, Article 43 of the Hague Regulations imposes significantly greater limits on the force that can be legally used by an occupier than by belligerents at war, requiring that the occupier "shall take all the measures in his power to restore, and ensure, as far as possible, public order and safety, while respecting, unless absolutely prevented, the laws in force in the country."[19] As occupier, it is argued, Israel shoulders responsibility for enforcing the rule of law in Gaza. Some go so far as to suggest that any terrorist activity originating there, such as the firing of mortars and rockets, is Israel's

---

17. Noura Erakat, "Collective Punishment or Not, Gaza Blockade Illegal (Part I)," October 22, 2010, available at http://www.thejerusalemfund.org/ht/display/ContentDetails/i/16694/pid/895.

18. Erakat, "It's Not Wrong, It's Illegal," p. 13.

19. Available at http://www.icrc.org/ihl.nsf/WebART/195-200053.

fault for failing to fulfill its obligations to maintain law and order.[20]

Moreover, the standard argument holds that as occupier Israel is restricted by the international laws of war to the use of law enforcement measures to respond to violence originating within Gaza, because a military response would be inherently disproportionate. Indeed, Erakat hints that even the use of firearms by Israel in the discharge of its obligation to police Gaza might be considered an "extreme measure."[21] If Israel were allowed under international law to use its military might rather than rely on law enforcement, she claims, it would put the Palestinian residents of Gaza in the impossible position of defending themselves against one of the world's most powerful armies "without the benefit either of its own military, or of any realistic means to defend itself."[22] Israel's contention that it is compelled to use military force in Gaza is, according to Erakat, nothing less than a "deliberate effort to shift" the interna-

20. Kattan, "Operation Cast Lead," pp. 109–110, and "The occupation of the Gaza Strip and the continued renouncement of responsibility," *International Law Observer* (2008), available at http://internationallawobserver.eu/2008/10/24/the-occupation-of-the-gaza-strip-and-the-continued-renouncement-of-responsibility/.

21. Erakat, "It's Not Wrong, It's Illegal," p. 15. (Erakat quotes from Marco Sassoli's paper "Article 43 of the Hague Regulations and Peace Operations in the Twenty-First Century.") See also Kattan, "Operation Cast Lead."

22. Erakat, "It's Not Wrong, It's Illegal," p. 20. Erakat references George E. Bisharat et al., "Israel's Invasion of Gaza in International Law," *Denver Journal of International Law and Policy*, 38:1 (2009), available at http://law.du.edu/documents/djilp/38No1/Bisharat -Final.pdf.

tional laws of war "by insisting that it can simultaneously be at war with the entity that it occupies."[23]

The Critique of the Occupation Argument

In reality, it is proponents of the standard argument who seek to shift the international laws of war, indeed to fundamentally rewrite them. Their view that Israel occupies Gaza cannot withstand scrutiny. It lacks foundations in the principles of international law and is at odds with common sense understandings of war and peace.

The challenge for Erakat and the standard argument that she champions is to show that despite the absence of boots on the ground in Gaza and notwithstanding that it does not perform the functions of government there, Israel nevertheless exercises effective control over and therefore occupies Gaza. To meet the challenge, Erakat misinterprets the significance of Israel's ability to deploy troops at will, and gives undue weight to its military operations in Gaza. And more generally, she substitutes the colloquial meaning of "effective control," namely, the ability to exercise significant influence, for the legal meaning under international law, which is to govern by force.

Erakat's argument that Israel's ability to deploy troops at will in Gaza is a mark of occupation is exposed to an immediate objection: "Military superiority over a neighbor does not itself constitute occupation. If it did, the United States would have to be considered the occupier of Mexico and

---

23. Erakat, "It's Not Wrong, It's Illegal," p. 14.

Canada, Egypt the occupier of Libya, Iran the occupier of Afghanistan, and Russia the occupier of Latvia."[24] In fact, Erakat suppresses the restricted circumstances under which international law regards the ability to deploy troops at will as an indicator of occupation.

The International Criminal Tribunal for the former Yugoslavia (ICTY) case she cites as the leading authority, *The Prosecutor v. Naletilic & Martinovic—Case No. IT-98-34-T* (2003), states that "to determine whether the authority of the occupying power has been actually established," several "guidelines provide some assistance." The court provided a list:

- The occupying power must be in a position to substitute its own authority for that of the occupied authorities, which must have been rendered incapable of functioning publicly.
- The enemy's forces have surrendered, been defeated, or withdrawn. In this respect, battle areas may not be considered as occupied territory. However, sporadic local resistance, even successful, does not affect the reality of occupation.
- The occupying power has a sufficient force present, or the capacity to send troops within a reasonable time to make the authority of the occupying power felt.

---

24. Avraham Bell and Justus Reid Weiner, "International Law and the Fighting in Gaza" (2008), p.18, available at http://www.jcpa.org/text/puzzle1.pdf.

- A temporary administration has been established over the territory; the occupying power has issued and enforced directions to the civilian population.[25]

No one of these guidelines is conclusive, none can be applied mechanically, and taken together they show that the core meaning of occupation under international law coincides with the common sense meaning and consists in subduing a civilian population by force and governing it by force.

Indeed, taken together, the guidelines elaborated in the ICTY case that Erakat takes as authoritative clearly indicate that Israel's relationship to Gaza falls well outside the legal definition of occupier. Despite the readiness of Israeli troops to defend against terrorist incursions and mortar, rocket, and missile attacks from Gaza, Hamas continues to govern Gaza; it has not been rendered incapable of functioning publicly; it has not surrendered or been defeated or withdrawn; and Israel does not administer Gaza or issue and enforce directives to the civilian population.

The circumstances, according to the ICTY Trial Chamber, under which the laws of occupation apply absent physical occupation shed additional light on the erroneousness of Erakat's view that Israel's ability to send troops into Gaza establishes its status as an occupying power. The court explained that the forced transfer of people and forced labor are prohibited from the moment civilians fall into the hands of the opposing power regardless of the stage of hostilities and irrespective of whether the hostile

---

25. *Prosecutor v. Naletilic* is available at http://www.icty.org/x/file/Legal%20Library/jud_supplement/supp42-e/naletilic.htm.

power has established an actual state of occupation as defined in Article 42 of the Hague Regulations. If a state has a degree of control that falls short of effective control, it will only be considered an occupier for the purposes of international law if that control is used to compel people to migrate or perform work involuntarily. In such circumstances, Geneva protections for occupied populations take effect, regardless of whether the hostile army has boots on the ground or exercises the functions of government.

Such circumstances, however, are not present in Israel's relation to Gaza. Israel is neither forcing anyone to leave Gaza nor compelling anyone to labor against his or her will. Again, the very ICTY opinion that Erakat cites as authority for the legal judgment that Israel—despite the absence of troops and the fact of Hamas's control of the government—occupies Gaza, explains why, under international law, Israel cannot properly be considered Gaza's occupier.

The ICTY opinion also indicates why Erakat is wrong to assert that Israel's military operations in Gaza indicate that it occupies Gaza. They are not, as Erakat contends, "continuous"; Operation Cast Lead has been the only major operation since 2005. More to the point, such military operations as Israel has conducted show that it does not occupy Gaza because Hamas has not surrendered, been defeated or withdrawn.

Erakat's contention that Israel exercises extensive forms of control over Gaza appeals to observable facts but depends on disregarding the clear application of the law to them. To be sure, as Erakat stresses, Israel does strictly limit the movement of people and goods in and out of Gaza, thus creating conditions that make it difficult for all Gazans to travel and for many to work. But extensive control is not, under the international laws of war, synonymous with effective control.

To begin with, Erakat wrongly asserts that Israel exercises *complete* control over Gaza's borders.[26] In fact, Egypt has controlled the Rafah crossing from Gaza to the Sinai Peninsula since Israel's disengagement in the summer of 2005 and maintained severe restrictions on the movement of goods and people through Rafah up until May 2011, when, following the February ouster of President Hosni Mubarak, it relaxed restrictions. In addition, the effects on movement and labor stemming from the forms of control Israel does exercise over Gaza are exactly the opposite of those that the ICTY opinion specifies as necessary, in the absence of boots on the ground and operation of the government, to trigger application of the laws of occupation. Instead of forced migration, Israeli policy causes Palestinians in Gaza to stay put; and rather than being subject to forced labor, Palestinians in Gaza find themselves, as a result of Israel's response to Hamas, underemployed or unemployed.

Such hardships, however, do not define occupation. In fact, they are among the consequences one would expect of war, even where the international laws of war are scrupulously observed. And Hamas not only believes that it is at war with Israel. It undertakes acts—firing mortar shells, rockets, and missiles at Israeli civilian populations; mobilizing for armed conflict; and constant planning and undertaking of terrorist incursions—that combine to meet the settled definition of aggression, namely acts

---

26. Erakat, "It's Not Wrong, It's Illegal," p. 12.

that threaten a state's territorial integrity or political independence.[27]

Although Hamas's precise legal status is open to question—Gaza is not a state, and Hamas came to power by overthrowing the Palestinian Authority—Hamas is the de facto ruler of Gaza and has exercised the functions of government there since June 2007. Notwithstanding its designation as a terrorist organization by the US State Department and the European Union, Hamas operates in Gaza a full range of ministries, a police force, a military, and makes and enforces the law. Consequently, Israel cannot be said to exercise effective control over Gaza in the legally relevant sense. Indeed, any attempt by Israel to exercise the "effective control" Erakat insists it still retains by imposing law and order on Gaza would quickly clarify that Israel lacks effective control in Gaza, in both the legal and the colloquial sense. To have prevented Hamas from launching rockets in the first place, as Erakat and others suggest it should have, would have required Israel to mount a full-scale invasion in 2007 in response to Hamas's overthrow of the Palestinian Authority. Such an action would have made Operation Cast Lead look like a minor border skirmish.[28]

At the same time, the firing of mortars, rockets, and missiles against Israel's civilian populations does not reflect a failure on Hamas's part to maintain law and order. Rather, it displays Hamas's determination to wage war

27. UN Charter, Article 2(4), available at http://www.un.org/en/documents/charter/chapter1.shtml.

28. Bell and Weiner, "International Law and the Fighting in Gaza," p. 18.

against Israel, indeed a kind of war that is strictly forbidden by international law.

Hamas reaffirmed its criminal intentions in the wake of Justice Richard Goldstone's April 1, 2011, reconsideration in the *Washington Post*, in which, as I have discussed in previous chapters, he withdrew the gravest charge his report leveled against Israel—that in Operation Cast Lead Israel had, as a deliberate policy, terrorized the civilian population of Gaza.[29] In addition, while applauding Israel for launching more than four hundred investigations of allegations of criminal wrongdoing arising from the Gaza operation, Goldstone expressed regret that Hamas had not undertaken a single one. When asked by the *New York Times* to respond to Goldstone, Hamas Justice Minister Mohammad al-Ghoul said that investigations were unnecessary because shooting rockets was " 'a right of self-defense of the Palestinian people in the face of the Israeli invasion and mass killing of Palestinians.' "[30]

Justice Minister al-Ghoul's statement is factually erroneous and legally wrong, but it gives expression to Hamas's criminal military strategy and objectives. Contrary to Minister al-Ghoul, there is no right under international law, in self-defense or otherwise, to deliberately target civil-

---

29. Available at http://www.washingtonpost.com/opinions/recon sidering-the-goldstone-report-on-israel-and-war-crimes/2011/04/01/afg111jc_story.html. For the scurrilous charge withdrawn by Goldstone, see "Report of the United Nations Fact Finding Commission on the Gaza Conflict," Part V, Par. 1690, available at http://www2.ohchr.org/english/bodies/hrcouncil/specialsession/9/docs/unffmgc_report.pdf.

30. Ethan Bronner and Isabel Kershner, "Israel Grapples with Retraction on UN Report," *New York Times*, April 3, 2011, available at http://www.nytimes.com/2011/04/04/world/middleeast/04 goldstone.html.

ians. At the same time, the shooting of rockets at civilians for which Minister al-Ghoul matter-of-factly takes responsibility and which the Goldstone report properly characterized as war crimes, did not take place in response to Israel's Gaza operation. Indeed, Hamas launched thousands of projectiles at Israeli civilians after Israel's withdrawal from Gaza in September 2005 and before Operation Cast Lead began in December 2008. Israel's Gaza operation was a response to Hamas attacks on civilians, not the other way around.

Given Hamas's officially declared intentions, its aerial assault over many years on Israeli civilians should not be surprising. Hamas's openly-declared aim in waging war against Israel is not in the first place to end a supposed occupation of Gaza or to break a naval blockade, but rather to annihilate Israel, as the Hamas Covenant makes abundantly clear: "Israel will exist and will continue to exist until Islam will obliterate it" (Preamble). "Hamas strives to raise the banner of Allah over every inch of Palestine" (Article 6). "There is no solution for the Palestinian question except through Jihad" (Article 13).[31]

The emptiness of the standard argument that Israel occupies Gaza was further confirmed in March 2011 by the UN Security Council.[32] Resolution 1973—adopted by a vote of ten in favor, none against, and five abstentions—authorized the use of military force to protect civilians against Muammar el-Qaddafi's fighters, imposed a no-fly

---

31. Available at http://avalon.law.yale.edu/20th_century/hamas.asp.

32. Eugene Kontorovich, "Is Gaza still Occupied?" *Jerusalem Post*, June 2, 2011, available at http://www.jpost.com/Opinion/Op-Ed Contributors/Article.aspx?id=223231.

zone across the entire country, and tightened the asset freeze and arms embargo established by UN Security Council Resolution 1970, while at the same time declaring that Libya was not and would not be occupied.[33] If, despite the extensive forms of control that NATO forces and the Arab League exercised over Libya under Resolution 1973, they could not be considered occupying powers, then it follows that Israel, which exercises lesser forms of control over Gaza cannot, consistent with international law, be deemed an occupying power of Gaza.

The Inherent Right of Self-Defense

The ultimate justification of Israel's naval blockade of Gaza—as well as of Operation Cast Lead and of the various measures that Israel continues to take to protect itself against Hamas mortar, rocket, and missile attacks and more—is its inherent right of self-defense. As I have emphasized, in exercising this right, Israel is obliged to honor the fundamental principles of the international laws of war. The principle of distinction requires combatants to distinguish civilians and civilian objects and prohibits attacking them, while also requiring combatants to distinguish themselves from citizens.[34] And the principle of proportionality bars attacks on legitimate military targets that knowingly produce harm to civilians and civilian objects that is excessive

33. Available at http://www.un.org/News/Press/docs/2011/sc10200 .doc.htm#Resolution.

34. ICRC, "Customary IHL," Chapter 1, available at http://www .icrc.org/customary-ihl/eng/docs/v1_cha.

in relation to the military advantage gained.[35] The proper legal question to ask in regard to any exercise of force is whether it conforms to the principles of distinction and proportionality. That would be true even if Israel were regarded as an occupying power.

The UN Charter, Article 51, declares, "Nothing in the present Charter shall impair the inherent right of individual or collective self-defense if an armed attack occurs against a Member of the United Nations, until the Security Council has taken measures necessary to maintain international peace and security."[36] International lawyers tend to adopt a narrow reading, contending that the right of self-defense can only be exercised in response to a direct attack, and that once the Security Council is seized of the matter states are barred from exercising their right absent Security Council authorization, even if the attack continues. Yet as Abraham Sofaer points out, "Advocates of a narrow interpretation of Article 51 disregard the substantial authority that exists among scholars and in state practice for a more flexible approach."[37] That more flexible approach is more consistent with the UN Charter's language, which recognizes that states' inherent right of self-defense is not conferred upon them by the UN or by international law. Instead, as Michael Walzer argues in his classic study, *Just and Unjust Wars*, nations' inherent right to defend themselves stems from the inherent right of the individuals who com-

---

35. ICRC, "Customary IHL," Rule 14, available at http://www.icrc .org/customary-ihl/eng/docs/v1_rul_rule14.

36. Available at http://www.un.org/en/documents/charter/chapter7 .shtml.

37. Abraham Sofaer, "International Security and the Use of Force," *Progress in International Law* (2008), p. 561.

pose states to judge what actions are necessary to defend themselves and provides the foundation of the modern state system and the international laws of war.[38]

Proponents of a narrow reading of Article 51, moreover, argue from the mistaken assumption that the more flexible interpretation of the inherent right of self-defense undermines international peace and security by inviting states to take the law into their own hands. But, as Sofaer stresses, "Self-defense is a key element in any sensible program to supplement the inadequate, collective efforts of the Security Council."[39] History provides ample evidence that the Security Council cannot be counted on to counter aggression swiftly and effectively. Consequently, exercise of the inherent right of self-defense is critical to upholding international order and vindicating the principle that aggression is criminal and will not be tolerated. At the same time, "Actions in self-defense should be judged by their reasonableness, as are issues of force in any other contests of law enforcement and national law."[40] Under the international laws of war, the decisive measures of reasonableness are the principles of distinction and proportionality.

In the last analysis, the question of the legality of Israel's blockade should be whether it distinguishes civilians and civilian objects and represents a proportional response to Hamas's declared jihad against it. As the Turkel Commission report argues and as the UN's Palmer report agreed, Israel's naval blockade conforms to the requirements of international

---

38. Michael Walzer, *Just and Unjust Wars* (New York: Basic, 2000), pp. 51–73 (in particular pp. 51–64).

39. Sofaer, "International Security and the Use of Force," p. 561.

40. Sofaer, "International Security and the Use of Force," p. 561.

maritime law, including allowing for the passage of humanitarian relief to the Gazan civilian population, and so does meet the requirements of proportionality.[41] Moreover, as an exercise of force aimed at preventing armed attacks by Hamas, Israel's naval blockade is considerably more protective of Gaza's civilians than the main alternative, a land invasion that would inevitably cause substantial civilian death and destruction because of Hamas's criminal military strategy of operating in civilian areas while disguised as civilians.

Erakat displays the argumentative extremes to which she is willing to go by contending that Israel's inherent right of self-defense does not apply to Palestinian aggression. Israel is barred from invoking a right of self-defense against Hamas fighters, she argues, because they are non-state actors. Her authority for this remarkable notion is the International Court of Justice's "Advisory Opinion on the Legal Consequences on the Construction of a Wall in the Occupied Palestinian Territory" (2004).[42] On this occasion, Erakat, alas, accurately reports the court's opinion. She fails to note, however, that this aspect of the opinion is widely regarded as bizarre, and is inconsistent with state practice, for example that of the United States for nearly a decade in its use of armed force against the Taliban in Afghanistan and Pakistan.

In her most comprehensive article on the blockade, Erakat maintains that the ICJ's advisory opinion on Israel's security barrier stands for two crucial propositions: "a

---

41. Turkel Commission report, pp. 100–102; Palmer report, pp. 40–44.

42. Available at http://www.icj-cij.org/docket/index.php?p1=3&p2 =4&k=5a&case=131&code=mwp&p3=4.

non-state entity cannot trigger Article 51 self-defense," and attacks that originate within occupied territory where the law of occupation applies distinguish the case of Gaza attacks on Israel from al-Qaeda's September 11 attack on the United States and therefore "[UN Security Council] Resolutions 1368 and 1373, which authorize the invocation of Article 51 self-defense against al-Qaeda, are distinct from, and non-applicable to, the Occupied Palestinian Territories."[43]

In regard to Erakat's first proposition, in providing that "nothing in the present Charter shall impair the inherent right of individual or collective self-defense if an armed attack occurs against a member of the United Nations," Article 51 does not require the attacker to be a state. Nor is that surprising. Even as the rise of transnational terrorists armed with weapons of mass destruction has confronted international law with novel and difficult questions, there have always been non-state entities, within states as well as in border regions of questionable territorial allegiance, that present threats to states' territorial integrity or political independence. And it is this criterion—whether an act presents a threat to a state's territorial integrity or political independence—and not whether the agent is a state or a non-state entity that determines whether the crime of aggression has been committed and states' inherent right of self-defense has been triggered. Subjecting one million citizens to the daily danger, and heavy civic and commercial dislocations, of mortar, rocket, and missile attacks as well as the ever present threat of terrorist incursion—as Hamas has done for many years to the civilians of southern Israel—threatens Israel's territorial integrity and

---

43. Erakat, "It's Not Wrong, It's Illegal," pp. 19–20.

political independence and so constitutes aggression by Hamas under the international laws of war.

Oddly, Erakat herself provides substantial scholarly authority to establish that she and the ICJ ruling on which she relies are in error to argue that "a non-state entity cannot trigger Article 51 self-defense." That ample authority, which contradicts the point in behalf of which she adduces it, is contained in her footnote 100:

> See e.g., Ruth Wedgwood, "The ICJ Advisory Opinion on the Israeli Security Fence and the Limits of Self-Defense" . . . ("The Charter's language does not link the right of self-defense to the particular legal personality of the attacker. In a different age, one might not have imagined that nonstate actors could mimic the force available to nation states, but the events of September 11 have retired that assumption."); See also Geoffrey Watson, Self-Defense and the Israeli Wall Advisory Opinion: The "Wall" Decisions in Legal and Political Context . . . (Watson argues that the ICJ's decision is "expansive and sweeping" and fails to conduct a proper analysis of law and fact.); See also Sean D. Murphy, Self-Defense and the Israeli Wall Advisory Opinion: An Ipse Dixit From the ICJ . . . ("First, nothing in the language of Article 51 of the Charter requires the exercise of self-defense to turn on whether an armed attack was committed directly by, or can be imputed to, another state. Article 51 speaks of the right of self-defense by a 'Member of the United Nations' against an armed attack, without any qualification as to who or what is conducting the armed attack. The 'ordinary meaning' of the terms of Article 51 provides

no basis for reading into the text a restriction on who the attacker must be.")[44]

Contrary to her apparent intention, Erakat highlights international law's convergence with the common-sense idea that states may exercise their right of self-defense against any actors, including non-state actors, that threaten their territorial integrity or political independence.

Although Israel does not occupy Gaza, it is worth noting that Erakat's second proposition, that attacks coming from occupied territory can never trigger a state's inherent right of self-defense, is also in error. Many articles in the Geneva Conventions that deal with the protection of civilians nevertheless recognize that in cases of military necessity humanitarian responsibilities do not cancel the right of self-defense. For example, the Geneva Conventions, Additional Protocol 1 (1977), Article 54, Sect. 5, concerns the obligation of occupying powers to prevent starvation and provide foodstuffs. It provides that "In recognition of the vital requirements of any Party to the conflict in the defense of its national territory against invasion, derogation from the prohibitions contained in paragraph 2 may be made by a Party to the conflict within such territory under its own control where required by imperative military necessity."[45]

---

44. Erakat, "It's Not Wrong, It's Illegal," pp. 19–20.
45. Available at http://www.icrc.org/ihl.nsf/full/470. For additional examples, see the Fourth Geneva Convention, Articles 18, 28, 49, 53, 55, 108, 143, and 147, available at http://www.icrc.org/ihl.nsf/full/380; and Additional Protocol 1, Articles 62, 67, and 71, available at http://www.icrc.org/ihl.nsf/full/470; and Additional Protocol II, Article 17, available at http://www.icrc.org/ihl.nsf/full/475.

Notwithstanding the responsibilities they owe civilians under their control, an occupying power retains its inherent right of self-defense. At the same time, and to repeat, a state's exercise of its inherent right of self-defense does not suspend international law, both because the inherent right of self-defense is a foundation of the international laws of war and because, in exercising it, states remain obliged to respect the principles of distinction and proportionality.

Reasonable and Unreasonable Disagreement

Reasonable people may differ over the soundness of the tactics Israel adopted to take control of the *Mavi Marmara* on May 31, 2010 and on whether Israeli commandos used inappropriate levels of force. Israel's Turkel report concluded that in general the commandos performed their jobs in a professional manner and conformed to the requirements of the international laws of war, while acknowledging that there were a few incidents for which they lacked sufficient evidence to make a determination.[46] The UN's Palmer report found that Israel's seizure of the *Mavi Marmara* involved the application of force that was "excessive and unreasonable."[47]

There is not, however, room for reasonable disagreement over whether Israel's naval blockade of Gaza is legal. One cannot argue coherently and in keeping with well-established principles of the international laws of war that

---

46. See http://www.turkel-committee.com/files/wordocs/8808re port-eng.pdf, p. 279.

47. Palmer report, p. 54.

Israel's naval blockade is inherently unlawful. As both the Turkel report and the Palmer report agree, the blockade is consistent with the principles of the international laws of war. In imposing a maritime blockade on Gaza that allows for the passage into it of goods that satisfy the civilian population's basic requirements, Israel is exercising its inherent right of self-defense against Hamas, the ruling power in Gaza, which is waging a religious war against Israel that aims at its total destruction.

CHAPTER FOUR

Conserving the International Laws of War

In the service of condemning Israel's conduct in Operation Cast Lead, the Goldstone report engaged in disreputable fact-finding and misapplied the relevant legal tests even as its mission lacked proper foundations in international law. And the standard arguments adduced in the Gaza flotilla controversy for viewing Israel's blockade of Gaza as unlawful prove on inspection to be unsound and insubstantial. The wide support garnered by the Goldstone report and the critique of Israel's blockade among international lawyers and progressive intellectuals testifies to their determination to subordinate the international laws of war to partisan politics and utopian legal visions.

Since the international laws of war stand or fall with their claim to transcend partisan posturing and rise above the political fray without getting lost in the clouds, and since these laws are a vital component of a freer, more peaceful, and more prosperous world order, most nations and certainly all liberal democracies have a vital interest in defending their integrity. That defense must devote considerable attention to the controversies in which Israel has become embroiled, because the sustained campaigns to criminalize Israel's exercise of its inherent right of self-defense are among the gravest abuses to which the international laws of war have been subject, and threaten to effect legal transformations that will impair the ability of all liberal democracies to defend themselves.

Indeed, in the guise of honoring the international laws of war the Goldstone report and many of those who argue that Israel's blockade of Gaza is illegal seek to rewrite them. The changes they champion shift responsibility for civilian losses away from terrorists and onto the states fighting them. The result is to reward those who, in gross violation of the international laws of war, deliberately efface the distinction between civilian and military objects, and to punish liberal democracies—in particular Israel and the United States—which expose their soldiers and civilian populations to heightened risk in the quest to wage war lawfully. Because rewarding behavior encourages more of it, the more such shifts in the international laws of war become entrenched, the more terrorists will operate within densely populated urban areas and target civilians.

In the short term, this might lead liberal democracies, in order to protect the other side's civilians, to expose their own soldiers and civilians to greater dangers. In the long term, reducing or dissolving terrorists' responsibility for the unintended harm to civilians and civilian objects that results from the terrorists' decision to take up positions among civilians and use civilian objects as weapons of war risks impelling liberal democracies to disregard the international laws of war as hopelessly impractical. This would undermine their own soldiers' sense of justice and honor and increase the peril to the other sides' civilians.

The growing influence of efforts to shift the international laws of war promotes the tendency among Israel's critics—lawyers and non-lawyers alike—to infer criminal conduct from the bare fact of civilian harm. This is certainly true of the Goldstone report and the Gaza flotilla controversy. The inference, however, relies on a magnification of combatants' humanitarian responsibilities toward the other sides' civilians and a disregard of the legitimate claims of military necessity that oblige states to use force to defend their citizens and territory.

As I have argued throughout, the main tests of criminality in the context of combat operations are distinction and proportionality. These principles require fighters to strike a reasonable balance between military necessity and humanitarian responsibility. The two can be mutually reinforcing—in the simplest case soldiers put their lives on the line to protect their fellow citizens—but often are in tragic tension as military forces seek to minimize the risk to their soldiers in pursuit of victory. Proper application of the laws of war involves an inquiry not only into the identity and suffering of civilians but also into tactics and strategy, battlefields and weapons, what troops and commanders knew and what they reasonably could have known. The principles of distinction and proportionality direct attention not only to combatants' responsibilities toward the other side's civilians but also to combatants' rights, and their responsibilities toward their fellow fighters, fellow citizens, and their state.

The inherent difficulties of applying distinction and proportionality are compounded when, as is the case with Hamas, one side unlawfully abandons the use of uniforms, disdains to carry its arms openly, hides amidst civilian populations, stores arms in ostensibly civilian facilities and, from within its own civilian areas, fires mortars, rockets, and missiles at the opposing sides' civilians. Such blatantly unlawful conduct deliberately exposes the terrorists' civilian populations to heightened risk of harm. But the international laws of war have been clear and should remain clear: even as the principles of distinction and proportionality continue in force, combatants who intentionally operate among civilians in order to gain military advantage remain legitimate military targets, and civilian areas and structures used by combatants for military purposes lose their immunity.[1]

In the aftermath of World War II, a great revolution in military affairs brought the conduct of war under vastly greater legal supervision. The revolution has accelerated over the last several decades and continues apace. In many respects it has made the inherently brutal enterprise of war more humane. At the same time, it has been accompanied by a politicization and idealization of the international laws of war that reward terrorism and weaken the right of liberal democracies to defend themselves. No cure or corrective to these dangerous developments will succeed that does not give close attention to the education of the next generation of lawyers, scholars,

---

1. ICRC, Customary IHL, Chapter 1, available at http://www.icrc.org/customary-ihl/eng/docs/v1_cha.

soldiers, and statesman. The young men and women who will assume responsibility for the preservation and elaboration of the international laws of war must be trained to respect the distinction between politics and law and to appreciate not only humanitarian responsibility but also military necessity. Consequently, conserving the international laws of war awaits a major reform of educational affairs.

About the Author

PETER BERKOWITZ is the Tad and Dianne Taube Senior Fellow at the Hoover Institution at Stanford University, where he chairs the Koret-Taube Task Force on National Security and Law and co-chairs the Jill and Boyd Smith Task Force on the Virtues of a Free Society.

He studies and writes about, among other things, constitutional government, conservatism and progressivism, liberal education, national security and law, and Middle East politics.

He is academic director of the Tikvah summer institute at the Hebrew University of Jerusalem, "The Jewish State: Democracy, Freedom, and Virtue." He served as a senior consultant to the President's Council on Bioethics, and is a member of the Policy Advisory Board at the Ethics and Public Policy Center, in Washington, DC.

He is the author of *Virtue and the Making of Modern Liberalism* (Princeton University Press, 1999) and *Nietzsche: The Ethics of an Immoralist* (Harvard University Press, 1995). In addition, he is the author of *Constitutional Conservatism*, forthcoming from Hoover Institution Press in 2012.

He is the editor of *The Future of American Intelligence* (Hoover Institution Press, 2005), *Terrorism, the Laws of War, and the Constitution: Debating the Enemy Combatant Cases* (Hoover Institution Press, 2005), the companion volumes *Varieties of Progressivism in America* (Hoover Institution Press, 2004) and *Varieties of Conservatism in America* (Hoover Institution Press, 2004), and *Never a Matter of Indifference: Sustaining Virtue in a Free Republic* (Hoover Institution Press, 2003).

In 2004, with co-editor Tod Lindberg, he launched Hoover Studies in Politics, Economics, and Society, a series of concise books on leading issues and controversies.

He has written hundreds of essays, articles, and reviews on many subjects for a variety of publications, including the *American Political Science Review, The Atlantic,* the *Boston Globe, The Chronicle of Higher Education, Commentary, Haaretz,* the *Jerusalem Post,* the *London Review of Books, National Review, The New Republic,* the *New York Post,* the *New York Sun, Policy Review, The Public Interest, Real Clear Politics,* the *Times Literary Supplement,* the *Wall Street Journal,* the *Washington Post, The Weekly Standard,* the *Wilson Quarterly, and* the *Yale Law Journal.*

He holds a JD and a PhD in political science from Yale University; an MA in philosophy from the Hebrew University of Jerusalem; and a BA in English literature from Swarthmore College.

About the Hoover Institution's
KORET-TAUBE TASK FORCE
ON NATIONAL SECURITY AND LAW

THE KORET-TAUBE TASK FORCE ON NATIONAL SECURITY AND LAW was formed to explore and provide answers to the many novel and difficult legal questions that arose for the United States in the wake of al-Qaeda's 9/11 attacks. The work of its members ranges widely, encompassing the Constitution, US criminal law, the international laws of war, military strategy, and domestic and global politics. The common goal is to clarify the vital principles that undergird, and develop practical proposals to reconcile, the claims of liberty and security in a dangerous world.

Current members of the task force include Kenneth Anderson, Peter Berkowitz (chair), Philip Bobbit, Jack Goldsmith, Stephen D. Krasner, Jessica Stern, Matthew Waxman, Ruth Wedgwood, Benjamin Wittes, and Amy Zegart.

Index

Books published by members and contributors to the
KORET-TAUBE TASK FORCE ON NATIONAL SECURITY AND LAW

Living with the UN: American Responsibilities
and International Order
Kenneth Anderson

Skating on Stilts: Why We Aren't Stopping
Tomorrow's Terrorism
Stewart A. Baker

Israel and the Struggle over the International Laws of War
Peter Berkowitz

Terror and Consent: The Wars for the Twenty-First Century
Philip Bobbitt

The Terror Presidency: Law and Judgment
Inside the Bush Administration
Jack Goldsmith

Detention and Denial: The Case for Candor
after Guantanamo
Benjamin Wittes

Law and the Long War: The Future of Justice
in an Age of Terror
Benjamin Wittes

Legislating the War on Terror: An Agenda for Reform
Edited by Benjamin Wittes

Eyes on Spies: Congress and the
United States Intelligence Community
Amy B. Zegart

Future Challenges in National Security and Law
Multiple Authors